WORKING LIGHT

The Wandering Life of Photographer Edith S. Watson

FRANCES ROONEY

CARLETON UNIVERSITY PRESS
IMAGES Publishing (Malvern) U.K.

Dedication

to Lois F. Watson,
who taught me as much about courage and dignity
as she did about Cousin Edith
and
to Meg, Mika, Max and Seelie, my little loves

Copyright © Frances Rooney, 1996

Published by Carleton University Press

Printed and bound in Canada

CANADIAN CATALOGUING IN PUBLICATION DATA

Rooney, Frances

    Working light : the wandering life of photographer Edith
S. Watson

(Women's experience series ; #8)
Includes bibliographical references.
ISBN 0-88629-273-5

    1. Watson, Edith S. 2. Women photographers—
Canada—Biography. 3. Canada—Pictorial works.
I. Title. II. Series: Carleton women's experience series ; #8

TR140.W37R66 1996   770'.92   C95-900805-5

Cover and interior design: Carrie Colton, Ottawa, ON.

Carleton University Press gratefully acknowledges the support extended to its publishing program by the Canada Council and the financial assistance of the Ontario Arts Council.

The Press would also like to thank the Department of Canadian Heritage, Government of Canada, and the Government of Ontario through the Ministry of Culture, Tourism and Recreation, for their assistance.

Published by Carleton University Press, 1996

This edition Images Publishing (Malvern) Ltd., 1996

Copyright © Frances Rooney, 1996

British Library Cataloguing in Publication Data

A catalogue record for this book is available from the British Library

ISBN 1 897817 83 5

Table of Contents

List of Plates

Acknowledgements

Three people, other than Edith, made this book possible. Frieda Forman showed me that first photograph. The woman at the Smithsonian who was interested enough to look for Edith in some very obscure places made it possible to find her family, her albums and her personal and business records. And because of Lois Watson's respect for her work, Edith's story and photographs have survived the 52 years since her death.

Lois has become very special to me. Her hospitality and the mutual affection which developed as I worked in her home made my research and those months a pleasure; her generosity enriched both me and the story told here. Lois introduced me to people, showed me places, told me family stories. She allowed me to make copy prints, she picked me up and took me back to the bus each day, she fed me, and when longer work hours became necessary, she let me stay in her home. During a time that was very difficult for her, she opened her life to me; she shared her knowledge of Bob's family with me. I am truly fortunate that she became and remains a friend.

Librarians and archivists are wonderful. My particular thanks to the hundreds of people who searched when all they had to go on was a name, when this project was still a question mark. Later, when the research became more focused, the staffs of numerous libraries went out of their way to be helpful and to make sure that I knew how interesting they found Edith and her story. Special thanks to the people at Nook Farm in Hartford, the Wood Memorial Library in South Windsor and the Connecticut State Archives. And, of course, my debt to that woman in the Smithsonian who put Edith's name together with a place, a town, is incalculable.

While I have put enough of my own money into this project to make a down payment on a substantial house, without the support of funders the work could not have continued. I received the largest Canada Council Explorations grant given to that time — it was my very first grant, and it made the essential travel and research possible. My thanks to Kate Hamilton for encouraging me to rework the application until I got it right and to the Council for taking a chance on a newcomer. I am also most grateful for the assistance of the Ontario Arts Council, the Lesbian and Gay Community Appeal of Toronto, the Canadian Research Institute for the Advancement of Women, and the Ontario Heritage Foundation.

I have worked in publishing for seventeen years, and have been writing for over 20, so I know how wonderful or awful the publisher-author relationship can be. From the beginning, my connection with Carleton University Press, and particularly with Jennie Strickland, has been a delight. No author could ask for more cooperation, more genuine interest, skill, enthusiasm, imagination, vision, foresight and just plain fun than has been my good fortune. This project has been a long long time in the works; to find such an ideal publisher truly feels like some kind of reward. Carrie Colton's long, hard and caring work on design is evident on the cover and every page.

Finally, there are the personal thanks. Some of these I can name, others know who you are. Pat Staton has been this project's best friend and my one-person cheering section almost from the beginning; I hope she knows how much I value her and her support. For many years John Plunkett and his predecessors helped me find the courage to keep going. My father, Frank Wiesman, did all he could to help, and for quite a while Lynne Martin was a major support. I am eternally grateful to the Ontario Institute for Studies in Education for laying me off three years ago — it was then that Rooney Editorial Services was born and my age of miracles began. Meg, Mika, Max and Seelie have loved me through every day and every inch of the way; without you it wouldn't have happened. And finally, to H.P., MCCT (especially Brent Hawkes, Walter Buchwalder, Toni Delabbio and Chris Hobbs) and all the people who have walked with me one day at a time since February 1994: thank you for my life.

Preface

When I told a friend that I couldn't believe my good fortune in having found Edith Watson, she said, "Sometimes we have to accept the presence of grace — or in this case, Edith — in our lives." She was right. What she didn't say was that grace — or in this case, Edith — is not always easy to live with.

In November, 1977 Frieda Forman of the Women's Educational Resources Centre at OISE showed me the xerox of a photo from a 1916 issue of *The Canadian Magazine of Politics, Science, Art and Literature*. The photograph showed a woman seated at a floor loom in House Harbor in the Magdalen Islands of Quebec. Unlike most photographers of the time, Edith Watson was credited. Frieda's "Why don't you see if you can find more of her stuff?" started me hunting.

Since a name was all I had, it was necessary to make certain arbitrary assumptions. My assumptions all made sense, they were all appropriate and logical in the circumstances. And they were all, without exception, wrong. My first hypothesis was that a photograph of a Canadian woman in a Canadian magazine had probably been taken by a Canadian. I went through all the usual reference books, I wrote to every major library and archive in the country, I combed old Canadian magazines. Within that first year I collected a file full of xeroxed photographs from the *Canadian Magazine* and

two articles in which those photographs were featured. But that was all I had. Would Edith Watson be traceable? Had she been Canadian? I was painfully aware that my efforts might have produced all there was to find. But I was hooked on Watson's gentle portraits of hard-working people; I decided to try the States.

The Smithsonian, the Library of Congress, the National Archives, the New York Public Library, the Schlesinger Library, the International Museum of Photography are wonderful places. But none of them had heard of Edith Watson. *Who's Who, Who Was Who, Notable American Women* and all their cousins turned up nothing. The *Art Index, International Index, Reader's Guide, Wellesley Index* and all *their* cousins referred me to hundreds of articles similar to those Watson illustrated, but Edith herself evaded me. Social historians, photographic historians, feminist historians and art historians were all very kind, intrigued and interested — but knew nothing of Edith Watson. City directories, directories of archives, directories of directories gave no clues. Indexes of countless biographies of Watson's contemporaries and colleagues gave me nothing but headaches.

After six more months I was ready to admit defeat. All my queries had been answered, and all the answers were negative. Then one day a letter arrived from a woman who worked in the basement of the Smithsonian who had been interested by my sketchy description of Edith Watson. I had said that I knew Watson had been active between

photo back - House Harbor, Magdalen Islands, Quebec

1914 and 1926, and that my search had started at 1910 and ended at 1930. The woman at the Smithsonian had continued the search, finding Watson in the 1954 *Who Was Who*. She apologized for not having found more.

It was enough. Edith Watson's birthplace no longer exists as a town, but a letter to the clerk of a neighbouring town brought the name of a possible relative. I wrote.

A month later a response came. Who was I? Why was I interested? How had I found cousin Edith?

I wrote back. And received no reply. I wrote again. Nothing. And again. Nothing. I decided that I had said something terribly wrong and had alienated the only possible source of more information; my heart sank at the thought of having come so close, only now to have to be content with secondary material and with the photographs, most of them poorly reproduced, that I could find in 60- or 70-year-old magazines.

Another year passed. Finally, in the fall of 1980 I could stand it no longer and wrote again. This time Lois Watson responded immediately. Her letter was cautious but straightforward. Bob Watson, her husband and Edith's cousin, had died shortly after my first letter arrived, and Lois had gone into shock for a year and been unable to write me until now. She said she was interested in the project and that there was a lot of material; enough, she thought, for a book. These included 8 x 10-inch glass negatives, 15 or 20 scrapbooks of Edith's photographs; watercolours and sketch

books; and many more notes and writings. Would I please write and let her know my plans.

I could hardly believe how much there was. I had thought that nothing could be worse than the blind search; I was wrong. Knowing there was so much to work with, and therefore so much to lose, was far worse.

We negotiated, each as cautious and, I think, as intrigued as the other, for several months. In July 1981, I went to Connecticut and spent four days with Lois Watson, getting acquainted and looking over the materials. She agreed to let me work with them, and with her, from September until Christmas. A generous Canada Council grant allowed me to take advantage of the opportunity.

Although the work was just beginning in earnest, the major part of the search was over. It had taken three and a half years to find Edith S. Watson.

That there was anything to find, that there is any story to tell is the result of Lois Watson's perseverance, her ability to recognize something special when she saw it, and her altogether too rare ability to respect the work of someone she didn't like. Lois had met Bob's cousin only a few times shortly after her marriage. She found Edith cold and uninterested in the domestic preoccupations of young newlyweds. She thought that Edith probably found her boring. Lois was crazy about Bob; Edith was at best neutral toward him. Said Lois to me, "He was just a man, and [Edith and Victoria Hayward] were … old maids." Too, there was the slight but nonetheless real awkwardness of Edith

and Bob's family connection. Bob was more than 40 years younger than his first cousin because his father, who had had seven children by his first wife, had remarried when he was 80 and sired three more children, of whom Bob was the youngest. And finally, there were the basic differences in their priorities: Lois was interested in home and family, Edith's immediate family had all died, she was preoccupied with art, travel, her partner in life and work, and herself.

All of which makes it all that much more remarkable that Lois saved as much of Edith's work as she did. The story of how she came to do so is a remarkable one.

Victoria Hayward, Edith Watson's partner of 32 years, had been living at their cottage on Martha's Vineyard for most of the time since Edith's death in 1943. Wild Acres, their house in Connecticut, had been unoccupied for the entire thirteen years, and looked it. In the yard, weeds had long since choked out most of the plants brought so lovingly from all over Canada. The windows were dark with dirt. The outside staircase to the second-floor studio lay in the grass, a tangled mass of planks; the roof was disintegrating. And vandals had been systematically looting the house. "Those relatives of Edith's," who had long been banned from Wild Acres for reasons no one remembered, obtained a court order to go into the house. Lois and Bob Watson, feeling more than a little like vandals themselves, went into the chaos of a home whose former inhabitants had known it as a far happier place.

F r a n c e s   R o o n e y

Empty frames from which Edith's and her sister Amelia's paintings had been cut littered the back porch. (The stolen paintings still show up at auctions, one here, two there.) The dining-room chairs were on the porch, too, waiting for the thieves' next truck. Inside, the sitting room was empty except for a bureau, a small desk and a high secretary-bookcase, while the living room contained only a victrola and an old square piano. In these rooms family photographs vied for space with the vines growing through walls, while vividly coloured patches on the faded wallpaper and shiny spots on dulled shelves told of pictures and knick-knacks already removed. A storage room, as yet undisturbed, contained two bureaus and several trunks whose labels shouted out from under the dust: France! Italy! St. John's! Montreal! Nassau! Quebec! Vancouver!

Nor, apparently, had the looters gone to the second floor. The hallway walls were still covered with paintings. The simple furniture was there, too: Amelia's bedroom set painted grey to match the walls; a narrow cot, a rod for clothes, a bureau and bookcase in the middle room; Edith's room distinguished by the presence of her prayer stand, surprisingly papish for an Episcopalian, in one corner. Queenie's back bedroom contained only a spool bed; the studio, added to the house in 1884 by Edith and Amelia, stood empty.

There was another storage room, whose contents included the remnants (and more) of the story of Edith's and Queenie's incessant travels: notebooks with a few scribbled pages headed Mexico, Havana, Anticosti, the Magdalens, Peter Verigin, Jobin, the Queen Charlottes; lists of expenditures, the budgets for their trips; tiny pairs of shoes still muddy from country roads; diaries, letters, a typewriter twelve inches square and six high, still in its leather-bound carrying case; presses for negatives, all kinds of developing equipment; and hundreds — thousands — of photographs and glass negatives.

The things the Watsons took away filled their extra barn. It would take two years of evening sortings to go through it all. Much was sold, much given away, and altogether too much, including bushel baskets of glass negatives, thrown away. Bob never did become very interested in his cousin's work. But as she sorted, Lois Watson realized that here was something special, and although not a Watson by blood, she could not allow this record to be obliterated. In the end, two rooms of her house were filled with Edith, Amelia and Queenie's belongings, arranged, organized and preserved as well as the demands of five adolescent sons and a working farm allowed.

When I arrived on her doorstep 20 years later, it was clear that Lois's enthusiasm had not faded. That July, as we looked each other over, she showed me all the material she then gave me permission to use in the fall.

Or so I thought. Six weeks into my stay, Lois decided to trust me with ... the rest. Out came boxes and a big old leather suitcase full of photographs and papers, another 5000 sheets of paper I later estimated, many of them covered in Edith's barely discernible scrawl, a few even cross-written. Sitting on the floor of an upstairs room, surrounded by press clippings, notes, diaries, photographs and paintings, and now up to my elbows in still more paper, I panicked. I had five weeks.

I became the mad xeroxer. Every evening I would take a bit of material with me — a diary, a scrapbook, a handful of letters — stop at the copy shop where I transferred buses, and stand at the self-serve machine for as much as an hour. I was miserable. I was hysterical. I was utterly happy.

What quickly became apparent was that Edith presented the researcher with almost an *embarras de richesses*. Hers were so many stories, her stories were windows to so many people, places and lives. She was born into an old New England family of merchants, printers and farmers. Her life coincided with the advancement of education for women in the U.S. and she lived much of that story, attending as she did one of the oldest female seminaries, which was founded in the late 1820s by education leader and pioneer Catherine Beecher. Edith pursued, very successfully, a profession in which there were more women than we tend to think (1890s census figures in both Canada and the U.S. indicate that about 15 percent of professional photographers in both countries were women) and she had friends who pursued occupations we have been taught to believe women simply did not undertake. She was a member of a virtual army of intrepid lady travellers, and was if anything more at home on the road or by a campfire than she was in her own house. No woman of leisure, she earned her living as a freelancer and supported herself and at times also her aged parents and her sister. She lived among hundreds of people of all walks of life: writers and artists, fishers and farmers, explorers and professional people. Her travels took her to houses and hotels of almost unbelievable luxury and to the simplest tent and open fire arrangements, from the Bahamas to northern Labrador, from eastern Newfoundland to the Queen Charlottes. Edith had an enviable business acumen, and she certainly has a place in the history of photography. Her story crosses that of the huge migrations across the Canadian-American border during the last third of the nineteenth century. She took part in the evolution of book, magazine and newspaper publishing in two countries. And she lived in a remarkable professional and personal partnership.

Deciding which part of her story to tell was in some ways the hardest thing to do and in other ways the easiest. Letting go, for the present at least, of some of those other themes in Watson's (or any other) life is, of course, torture for a researcher. But through, around and dominating Edith's story are the Canadian photographs. And the more I looked at them, the more I grew able to see them, the more clear it became that what was needed was a way for them to tell their own tale. The original manuscript included much more and specific information on Edith's family life and her artistic and business matters. That information, wonderful as it all is, and necessary as it would be to a more academic book, had to go if we were to include more than a few photographs. In fact, the original concept was to produce a full-length biography with twelve photographs. While there certainly is enough information for such a book, and while the exploration of all the facets of Edith's life could keep a researcher happily working for a lifetime, economics has necessitated that either the words or the photographs go. Like most writers, I love my own words like children, and the letters, reviews, and editors' comments that do not appear here would have added much to the story, but a book about Edith — especially the first book — that is all tell and almost no show would clearly be going about the whole thing backwards. The manuscript here is a quarter the length of the first manuscript. There are ten times the photographs. The tradeoff is worth it.

As the work progressed, several things happened that made me wonder just what Edith's own part was in this complex weave. At first I had considered this my own research project. After a short while I just wasn't so sure anymore. Sometimes I've felt driven, used, or even possessed by some kind of momentum that seemed to have little if anything to do with me and a great deal to do with Edith and the extremely forceful personality she was. Since I'm a relatively practical sort and not given to seeing the supernatural in things, this realization came as something of a shock.

But the power was there. In the preservation, against all odds, of so much material. In my inability and that of the woman at the Smithsonian, also in the face of great odds, to give up. And in the sheer force of coincidence.

Frieda Forman had showed me that first photograph, I discovered when I went back to my day book, on November 9: Edith Watson's birthday. I started to write the text on December 22: the date of her death. I grew up 60 miles from Wild Acres, and my mother's mother's family came from Hadlyme, a tiny village in Connecticut: the same town, it turned out, where several of Edith's mother's mother's relatives lived. Edith was descended from John Rogers, who migrated to Connecticut just before 1700 and founded the Rogerine Quakers. My grandmother Evelyn Rogers was descended from the same person. Edith Watson spent the equivalent of several years in her adopted Canada. I left New England to move to Canada more than half my life ago. When I told my brother that Edith had sold 300 photographs to *National Geographic*, of which six had eventually been published, he pulled out the only two copies of the magazine he had saved from his childhood collection. Both had obviously contributed to many school projects; several pages in each were ribbons of margin left after the removal of pictures. And in both, intact, were photographs by Edith S. Watson.

It looks, too, as if Edith had planned to have her story told. Not only did she keep numerous scrapbooks of her life and work, in the manner of many a Victorian woman, she scribbled notes in their margins that amount to pathways for the chronicler. Only one of her diaries has survived, that of a three-week trip around Connecticut and Massachusetts in 1884 with her donkey, Jaffa ("total cost of my trip, $5.00"). Of this I cannot help but feel a bit of guilty relief: her handwriting is barely decipherable. But some of the diaries of those around her, her mother, her sister, and Victoria Hayward, have survived, and these are wonderfully informative.

Perhaps most important, Edith was a very self-conscious artist who had no "proper" Victorian qualms about seeing her name in print. At a time when publishers for the most part considered photographers unnotable fillers of empty space, she insisted on — and got — not only top prices, but credits printed on her work. Without the prices, she would have had to do some other kind of work, perhaps teach painting as Amelia Watson did. Without the photographs, credits and Edith's wish to be known and remembered, she would have been irrevocably lost in the abyss of Anon.

Still, no life can be fully known, not even a professional life, and many mysteries remain. Two of these, both of which arise from Edith's Newfoundland travels, particularly intrigue me.

One question often comes up about people who travelled Newfoundland and Labrador at the end of the last century and the beginning of this one: Did they know Wilfred Grenfell, the legendary medical missionary and author whose name, after his arrival there in 1892, became synonymous with the establishment of medical care in Labrador? I searched Edith's photographs and records for indication of Grenfell. Finding none, I decided that she either hadn't known him or had left no record of their acquaintance — which seemed unlikely given the indelible impression he made on everyone who encountered him. Then, as I wandered through snapshots of Edith and Queenie, there was one of them and a white-haired man. I had missed it in part because it was obviously taken in a southern garden and not in Labrador. On the back, in Edith's hand, is written: "Edith, Queenie and Dr. Grenfell. Miami, Fla. on his birthday." How, when and where had Edith met him? How well did she know him? How many years did their acquaintance or friendship span? Will these questions ever be even partially answered?

The second mystery arose in Toronto and headed straight for St. John's. Lorraine Filyer worked for me in the library at Mount Allison University when she was a student and I was at my first job. Fourteen years later, I worked for her at *This Magazine*, of which she was managing editor. I showed her some of Edith's photographs one day, and to my shock she said she'd seen one of them before. A friend had it over her fireplace. The friend, a Newfoundlander, had gone home to visit

Edith, Queenie and Dr. Grenfell. Miami, Fla. on his birthday

Photograph by Edith Beach

and seen a show of photographs in a little gallery in a rundown old St. John's storefront. The photographs had been taken by an anonymous photographer who travelled the coast of Newfoundland and Labrador for many summers at the turn of the century, and who, rumour had it, spent winters in New England with his lady love. He had left many photographs around the area, and they had now been collected for this showing. Since the photograph was clearly Edith Watson's, it seemed to me that this mysterious traveller had in fact not been a man at all but an intrepid young woman.

Almost immediately after this conversation I left Toronto for several months. As I remember it, when I returned, I asked Lorraine to introduce me to her friend so that I might see the photograph and ask her about the show and the storefront gallery. Lorraine didn't remember our conversation, nor did she recall the photograph. I never met the woman, never found out about the show. I wondered if it was all a particularly vivid dream. Had it been wishful thinking on my part? Had Lorraine forgotten?

While preparing this manuscript for the printer, I mentioned our (real or imagined) conversation to Lorraine. She said that she remembered it clearly, wondered why I hadn't contacted her friend, and gave me the woman's name — again, apparently. As soon as the manuscript and photographs are with the publisher, I will contact the woman. This part of the story may not be finished.

The photographs in these pages show many people's homes and families. The images will remind people of old family photographs — some of which Edith took. I would be intrigued and pleased to hear from people, to find out how far Edith's web extends. I see this book not as an end but as a beginning, a part in a process of connections.

For connecting — with people, places and the history of this country — is what a book of this nature is ultimately about. As I researched and wrote it, Lois Watson said repeatedly, in a most un-New England lady-like manner which increases the emphasis, "I couldn't throw all that stuff out. Those two women loved that country so damned much." The life, the travels, the photographs make this love abundantly clear.

Queenie (left) and Edith at Wild Acres, 1942. The staircase to the studio is at the left of the picture. This is the last photograph of Edith
Photograph by Mary Beach

The Wandering Life of

WORKING

Photographer Edith S. Watson

LIGHT

FRANCES ROONEY

Edith fishing on the French River, Ontario, 1920s

Photographer unknown

Working Light

e dith Watson spent virtually her entire adult life as a travelling freelance photographer. Although during the 1880s she exhibited and sold paintings with her sister Amelia, by the early 1890s she was making the transition to the camera. Her wanderings took her throughout New England, New York, Pennsylvania and then the entire eastern seaboard of the United States, to Nassau and the Bahamas, Mexico, the Yucatan, Cuba and Bermuda. But her primary focus, and the subjects of the overwhelming majority of her photographs, were the rural people of Canada and the then Crown Colony of Newfoundland and Labrador. Starting in Nova Scotia and Newfoundland and working her way across the country year by year, she recorded what she saw in the thousands of photographs she sold to magazines, newspapers, books, manufacturers, provincial governments, hotels, and railroad and shipping lines, and gave to friends in Canada, the U.S., the U.K. and Bermuda. For the first two decades she usually worked alone. For the last 32 years of her life, she lived and worked with Bermudian writer Victoria Hayward.

During her brief periods at home at Wild Acres in East Windsor Hill, Connecticut, Edith recorded her art and her wanderings. She made numerous scrapbooks of reviews and press notices of her work and activities and of events in places she visited. She kept extensive business and personal accounts. She collected the books she and Amelia illustrated, and those their friends wrote. And she assembled her favourite Canadian photographs, 1700 of them taken primarily between 1894 and 1928, in photo albums. It is those albums that are represented here.

Edith Sarah Watson was the youngest of Reed and Sarah Watson's four children. Both Sarah's family, the Bolleses, and the Watsons had been among the first settlers in Connecticut. Sarah's family were printers and political activists in Hartford, which would during Edith's lifetime become the insurance capital of the east, and which stood just across the Connecticut River from East Windsor Hill, where the Watsons were merchants, lawyers and farmers. Sarah's father, one of two founders of the *Hartford Times* in 1817, had subsequently gone on to work in his brother's firm, Bolles and Houghton, predecessor of both Houghton Mifflin publishers and its printer, the Riverside Press. Although Reed was primarily a tobacco farmer, he worked intermittently as a printer for the Bolleses in Cambridge and courted Sarah Bolles there.

The Watsons appear to have been interested in art, botany, each other's lives and activities, a socially demanding religion run by a gentle God, and in economics. The overwhelming impression is of deep affection, Yankee ingenuity and shrewdness, a strong sense of the roles of work and play in the formation of a satisfactory life on earth, and a distinct lack of interest in earthly deprivation as preparation for life after death. Despite the worries of dependence on an extremely fragile crop and the loneliness of long separations while Reed worked in Cambridge in the times of a poor harvest or weak market, life at Wild Acres seems to have been remarkably pleasant. This sense is underlined by a scribble on the title page of Edith's *Instruction in Latin* (whose title she altered to *Destruction in Latin*): "We never could have loved the earth so well if we had had no child hood in it — George Eliot."

The children certainly all thrived. Rosa, born in 1853, was the intellectual gem of the family. Reed's brother Sereno, who had earned first a Ph.D. and then an M.D. at Yale, worked with Asa Gray at his Herbarium at Harvard and edited his *Botany of the United States* after Gray's death. At age sixteen, Rosa joined her uncle as a junior colleague. In the four short years before she died both her family and the academy took note of her brilliance as a botanist. Her botanical collection remained at Harvard until 1915 when it was given to the Hartford Scientific Society.

Edith at 5, 1866

Photographer unknown

Mourning card Edith and Amelia made in memory of Rosa

Less is known of Donald, born two years after Rosa. According to family stories Don was retarded and stayed on the farm all his life, but this intimation of parental heartbreak and childish misery could hardly be in greater contrast to the obviously bright, joyous child who wrote his uncle Sereno about winter skating and sledding parties and about studying Latin and algebra. Circumstances are unclear, and records provide virtually no information, but he may have had some kind of accident, for in 1875, also at twenty, Donald too was dead. This was probably the darkest time of Edith's life.

Of Amelia's birth in 1856 Sarah wrote to her own mother, "The baby is perfect, and arrived the exact day I predicted. Here is a lock of her hair." Amelia was also beautiful, as Edith's many photographs of her attest. Like Rosa, her talent for painting became evident early, and also like Rosa, she established a professional reputation before she was out of her teens. She and Edith were lifelong companions; their stories are intertwined.

Amelia was five by the time Edith was born. Sereno played a significant part in Edith's life, too. He sometimes taught photography as well as botany at Harvard, and she learned the technical parts of photography from him. Although she showed early talent, she would be over 30 before it became clear just where her immense curiosity, her dual passions of travel and photographic art would take her.

Physically, Edith most resembled her sister Rosa. But where Rosa had been soft featured, with shiny wavy brown hair, Edith's jaw was too strong and set, her brown hair too dull and straight, her glance more direct, shrewd and perceptive than was generally considered appropriate for a young lady. Temperamentally, she was unique in the family. From the beginning she was strong willed, quick tempered, self-contained and ambitious. Fortunately, first her gentle family and later Victoria Hayward were able not only to foster and appreciate her as she was, they were able to smooth her dealings with the world — and its with her.

Family life was relaxed and comfortable, if financially precarious. Rosa and Sarah wrote letters to each other which they delivered in the mailbox, Don played among the farm animals and birds, Edith and Amelia created faraway fantasy worlds in corners of the property and in the gulley that ran behind the house — the same places Edith would later put the plants she brought back from Canada.

All four children received their early education from Sarah. They may then have attended their uncle Edmund Watson's school. Edith spent four years at Hartford Female Seminary (HFS), one of the oldest educational institutions for women in the country. It may be that she went not only for the rigorous education there but to relieve the newly subdued atmosphere at home, for by the time Edith was 15, both Rosa and Don had died and Amelia was in Saratoga Springs, New York, where she would spend five years teaching at Temple Grove Seminary (the longest separation the sisters would experience). Whatever her reasons for going to HFS, the principles of friendship among women and of doing for and relying upon oneself, established at home and nurtured at school, would provide the working bases of Edith's entire life.

Amelia returned home in 1883, a year after Edith's graduation. She had already had several successful shows in New England and Saratoga. By mid-decade the reviews were noting that Miss Edith Watson had joined her sister in showings and sales.

Their schedule was a demanding one. Shows routinely included more than a hundred pieces. Edith conducted the business negotiations, while both sisters hung the shows, attended openings, consulted with prospective buyers and then took the paintings down, often only to pack them and move to another city a day or two later. This usually meant a bus ride for both the women and the paintings, and getting crates to and from bus stations at both ends. Although it amounted to a lot of scrambling for a $5 sale here, a $10 sale there, the numerous sales and enthusiastic reviews made it worthwhile, satisfying and profitable.

In 1884 the sisters designed and had built a studio at the north side of the house. The two glass walls made quite a local sensation; almost as unusual was the outside staircase in addition to access from the second floor of the house. The studio became the heart of the house as soon as it was finished. Both sisters worked there, and Sarah and Reed frequently visited in the evenings. Amelia painted portraits of her parents there, and some of Edith's earliest photographs show them by its fireplace.

Three years later, Sarah bought a cottage at Oak Bluffs, on Martha's Vineyard, the resort island five miles by ferry from both Cape Cod and Nantucket. The cottage would be a retreat for the women of the family until 1956, when it was sold to help support Victoria Hayward in a nursing home. It was also within sight of the Martha's Vineyard Summer Institute (MVSI), a summer school whose art department Amelia headed for many years.

As their circle of artistic friends grew, the sisters began to conduct shows and sales of their

Amelia at Martha's Vineyard while she was teaching at MVSI

Edith at 30, about the time she started her travels to Canada

Photograph by Fred Warner

work at Wild Acres. Often, four or five women would arrive several days early or stay for a few days after the Saturday shows. Neighbours would see them wandering the field-like grounds, engrossed in discussion, stopping as Edith pointed out the rocks and plants she had begun to collect and take home.

Many of the people who would be central to the sisters' lives and careers attended the Wild Acres showings. The Watsons' cousins, the Beaches, Mary who later took up photography as a serious amateur, and Edith and Frances who for years conducted a small publishing business out of their West Hartford estate, were regulars. Sereno Watson attended a few times before his death in 1892. Among frequent guests were members of Nook Farm, not a farm at all but an intellectual community in Hartford whose residents included Mark Twain, Harriet Beecher Stowe and the suffragist and women's rights speaker Katherine Houghton Hepburn (whose daughter of the same name would become even better known in her time than her mother was in her own). Regulars at the Watsons' included Will Gillette, producer, playwright and the actor who created Sherlock Holmes on the stage, a lifelong friend and (given the affection in his letters to her) perhaps suitor of Amelia's, and Fred Warner, renegade son of humorist Charles Dudley Warner. In the mid-1890s Fred would leave Hartford permanently to photograph the American west and explore the mountains of British Columbia and Alaska. The one

remaining photograph of Edith as a young woman is one of his portraits.

Several of the guests were painters met on the Vineyard or colleagues of Amelia's from MVSI, people such as botanist Edward S. Burgess and his wife Ruth Payne Burgess, and the founder of Wheelock College, Mary Wheelock.

Other attendants included popular poets Celia Thaxter and Eveleen Stein, poet and playwright Anna Hampstead Branch, writers Mary Wister (granddaughter of actress and abolitionist Fanny Kemble) and her brother Owen, and Helen Hunt Jackson, author of the Saxe Holme stories. Also among the regulars were zoologist and physiologist and former classmate of Edith's Dr. Mary Victoria Lee and Amelia's friends from Tryon, the former head of the Children's Hospital in New York, Dr. Bedell, and her companion Miss Angel.

Perhaps the most important visitors were Margaret Warner Morley and Helen Hyde. Margaret, a niece of Will Gillette, was an internationally known expert on both agriculture and beekeeping. When the British government decided to explore the agricultural prospects of the British West Indies, they asked her to conduct the investigations. She wrote many books, mainly on the physical and social lives of bees and wasps. It was as an outgrowth of this work that she decided to write her remarkably candid sex book for young people. She was Amelia's closest friend. Margaret's companion Constance Snow and Victoria Hayward later became particularly good friends.

In 1896 Margaret Morley went to Nova Scotia, New Brunswick and Prince Edward Island to write her book *Down North and Up Along*, whose title is taken from nautical terms common in that area. Edith and Amelia went with her. Amelia is the companion "M" (Minnie) referred to throughout the book. *Down North* was Edith's first commissioned book-length photographic assignment. Its dozen illustrations, made from 2 x 2-inch prints, comprise some of her most delicately executed work, and are an early indication of her compositional talent.

It was through Margaret that Edith met John Muir, naturalist, mountain climber, explorer of glaciers and jungles, white water canoeist and founder of the Sierra Club and the U.S. National Park system. When he decided to publish accounts of his walk from the Gulf of Mexico first to and then around the Great Lakes, he asked Edith to illustrate the books.

Helen Hyde was a latecomer to these gatherings. When they began she was living in Japan, where she studied painting and lithography and became extremely popular with Japanese audiences. When she returned to the U.S. after several years, she lived mainly in San Francisco, but travelled extensively, visiting Wild Acres whenever possible. Her work created a sensation, for she not only introduced certain Japanese techniques into North American art, but revolutionized lithographic techniques. Edith and Amelia were both personally and professionally devoted to Helen

Hyde and she to them; of all the deaths of friends the sisters experienced, hers in 1928 would be second in impact only to Margaret's the next year.

During the 1890s, reviewers began to note that the settings of Amelia's paintings had branched out to include Florida, North Carolina and Nova Scotia. Edith, on the other hand, was contributing scenes from Bermuda, Nova Scotia and Newfoundland. The sisters' paths had begun to diverge.

The two would continue to go many of the same places, and on many occasions they travelled together. But Amelia tended to wander to the south, while Edith went east, north and west. Amelia's trips were much more tame than Edith's. She travelled with friends, Edith usually went alone. Amelia visited old friends along the way, Edith met new ones. And Amelia did something that Edith never considered: she built her own house, her second home.

Will Gillette's retreat, Thousand Pines, outside Tryon, North Carolina, was to become the centre of an artists' colony in the town. Amelia bought a piece of land adjacent to Gillette's and built her house, Under the Tupelo, in 1894. She spent several months there each year until 1930.

Also in 1894, Houghton Mifflin decided to publish a two-volume limited anniversary edition of Thoreau's *Cape Cod*. The publisher commissioned Amelia to illustrate it.

She took her own copy of the book and, following Thoreau's route with a friend, wandered

Amelia c. 1900

Sarah Watson

the Cape sketching her impressions along the way. She made several large watercolours; others, many no bigger than a postage stamp, she drew in the margins of her book. Houghton Mifflin reproduced these as she drew them — marginal sketches. The result is a work luminous with Thoreau's spirit and Amelia's art. Reviewers and readers raved about the book for years after its publication.

It was a euphoric time for Amelia. She was famous, financially secure and among good friends.

While Amelia consolidated her reputation at home, Edith flung herself into the wanderings that would occupy the rest of her life. The pattern she established in the 1890s would remain steady until it was disrupted by the First World War. And she went to two drastically different kinds of places: Newfoundland and Labrador at first, then gradually across Canada to Vancouver Island and the Queen Charlottes, on the one hand, and Bermuda on the other.

In many ways, Bermuda was the perfect place for an artist to spend several months each year. A paradise for the rich, it was not a place many middle-income people went, and away from the luxury hotels, the living could be pleasant, relatively inexpensive and very profitable.

Each year, starting in 1898, Edith rented a studio where she lived and worked, usually from shortly after Christmas until February or March. She painted small watercolours, often several versions of one scene, some identical, some with variations in colour or mood. A bright inviting beach scene in one picture might become the foreboding setting of an approaching storm in another. Sometimes she added a small boat on the horizon or replaced a tree with flowering shrubs.

At first Edith took her work to managers of the large hotels like the Bermudiana, and after their scrutiny, arranged to show it on the premises. Before long, the hotels were writing her each autumn to request her return and arrange the dates for her shows. It was common practice for a section of the lobby to be set aside for the visiting artist, who would open with an all-day show on Monday, then be available for questions and conversation during the mornings until Friday. Not only did prospective buyers have the chance to look over the work as they passed to and from their rooms, they could meet and talk with the artist, buy what was then available, or set up future commissions.

Edith met many of her Bermudian friends this way. She sold hundreds of paintings and photographs, and her growing reputation and many and varied acquaintances spread her work all over North America and England and provided her with contacts as widespread as her work.

At about the same time she started passing winters in one of the most elegant and luxurious resorts in the world, Edith began to spend her summers in fishing villages that cling precariously to the thin shelves of rock along the tempestuous North Atlantic. Shortly after Easter, which she tried to spend at Wild Acres, Edith would set out.

New Englanders of this time were relatively aware of Canada and Newfoundland and Labrador. Many had family ties: people of British background often with former United Empire Loyalists ("Tory traitors" to the Americans), thousands of French-Canadian migrants with those left behind in Quebec, and Portuguese fishers of the east coast with relatives in Labrador. The Canadian and U.S. fisheries were closely linked. During this period, the Canadian government hired itinerant preachers and outfitted trains which then criss-crossed the eastern and mid-western states recruiting farmers. Literary magazines, to several of which middle-class families, and certainly the Watsons subscribed, printed many travel articles and ponderings about Canada.

And transportation was fast and easy. Numerous small train lines vied for passenger trade in both Canada and the U.S. Even faster than the trains were the ships of the Maritimes-based steam lines that ran between New England and Maritime ports. Edith could go from Wild Acres to Halifax in one (albeit long) day. From there she took the train to North Sydney, then the overnight mail-and-passenger boat to Port aux Basques.

She went to Newfoundland first as a painter. Local newspapers would announce her arrival, note which family she was boarding with, where she planned to work and how long she was staying.

But photography had grown increasingly important to Edith during her twenties and early thirties. Her extant Canadian photographs date from 1894,

not long before this poem that accompanied a camera given to her for Christmas in 1897.

Tra, la, la, la, la, la,
I've come to be your Camera!
Where thou goest far and near
I will go, all through the year.

All your friends and dear relations
And your many sweet creations
In your wanderings to and fro
Where the waters ebb and flow

Where the fishing streams meander
And the fishes leap at random
Hill and valley, as you wander
I will be your dear companion.

And the dreamiest, sweetest, loveliest,
On my camera reflected,
Shall be brought to "Paw and Maw",
And Minnie ha ha, Tra la la!

By the time her mother gave her this camera, newspaper reports were noting that "Miss Edith Watson, the well-known water color painter," had "brought her camera with her this season." By the turn of the century they were referring to her as "Miss Edith Watson, the well-known camera artist."

The photographs plot her path. Travelling on ships whose names have been lost or aboard the *Invermere* or the *Kyle*, Edith wandered from St. John's or Port

Reed Watson

Edith and Queenie on a trip to Labrador. Although the photograph is marked "on board the SS Lintrose" life preservers are from the SS Kyle, and Edith and Queenie frequently travelled aboard the Kyle. The photograph is dated 1912, but both women are clearly much older. Probably 1930s

Photographer unknown

aux Basques along the south coast, then up the west coast past the icebergs in the Strait of Belle Isle to Battle Harbor, Labrador, and north from there.

Edith fell in love with the land and its people. In many ways she was more at home in this rugged place than she was in refined Connecticut. She made friends easily, she lodged for many weeks each year with a few families, several days at a time with others. And her camera was omnivorous. Her photographs show the people she met at all their ordinary activities. Adults and children, working and resting, content, resigned, angry, let her into all aspects of their lives. She had found her medium.

And she had found her product. At first she gave prints to friends, sold some to acquaintances. Before long she was illustrating the booklets that local steamship and railway lines used for promotion. She illustrated the books of friends. The largest addition to her income came from companies whose products she photographed. She sold prints to the companies whose rope rigged the ships she travelled on, to the manufacturers of the buckets she used at village wells, to the exporters whose barrels she photographed being made. She exchanged photographs for passes on railroad and steamship lines: the small Maritime railroads as well as the CPR and CNR, the local ferries as well as the Cunard line. In work where constant travel was the basic component, these exchanges were invaluable. Also, since arrangements did not involve exclusive reproduction rights, she was free to sell the same photographs elsewhere. And she did: to individuals, to newspapers, to other companies.

Shots of particular technical quality she kept for the manufacturers of photographic equipment. Until after the First World War, Kodak and Ansco offered photographers cash for one-time use of their work, or double the cash payment in chemicals and paper. Frontenac Photo Supply bought large quantities of Edith's work until the late 1930s. Edith collected materials until she had a glut, then accepted cash payment for her work.

Meanwhile, Sarah and Reed were getting old. While Edith travelled, Amelia continued to teach and exhibit in New England and New York. The Houghton Mifflin edition of *Cape Cod* and the avid collecting and publicizing of her work that Will Gillette had started in 1898 enabled her to spend most of her time with them — as long as Edith continued to bring in the major portion of the family income. When Reed died in 1905, she was in Nassau and could not return home. Sarah lived another five years; during this time intervals of good health alternated with periods of severe indigestion and uncomfortable sleeplessness. Edith spent as much time at home during those years as she could, and was at Wild Acres when her mother died shortly before Christmas in 1910.

The 49- and 54-year-old sisters had every reason to believe that their lives would continue, with somewhat more freedom of movement than in recent years, along their established patterns. Amelia's did. Edith's was about to undergo drastic personal and professional change.

In the spring of 1911 friends in Bermuda introduced Edith to 35-year-old Bermudian journalist Victoria Hayward. The two made friends quickly. When Edith returned to Canada they corresponded. That autumn Victoria visited Edith in East Windsor Hill. Next spring, when Edith arrived in Bermuda, Queenie, as Victoria was called, moved in with her. They lived and worked together for the rest of Edith's life.

It was an ideal emotional and working relationship. Physically and tempermentally, Queenie was similar to Amelia, and in some ways Edith's opposite. She was tall, agile except when impeded by a bad leg that bothered her periodically during most of her life, and strikingly pretty. She was much less serious about herself and her work than Edith, and was socially easy. She had none of Edith's craving for immortality, and none of her compulsion to accomplish.

In other ways they were remarkably similar. Few people could have kept up, good naturedly, with Edith's travel schedule. Queenie loved it. She was interested, with Edith, in the working lives of the people they met. She and Edith were both addicted to islands and the sea.

In still other ways they were complementary. Edith's drive needed Queenie's calm. Her seriousness needed Queenie's humour. Her temper needed the balance of Queenie's ready sense of the absurd. Queenie wrote articles to accompany Edith's photographs and logged the photos for future reference; Edith conducted most of the business negotiations of their partnership. Edith was a much better photographer than Queenie was a writer, as editors never

tired of pointing out, and when commissions fell through it was usually because the article was too little or too late or both.

Edith needed to be recognized as an artist, Queenie did not. Nor did she mind that Edith's professional virtues were often mentioned in contrast to her own inadequacies. Edith's fierce independence found its rest and home in Queenie.

A second important change, this one purely professional, came from a revolution in the magazine industry; its impact on Edith and Queenie's careers became evident during the First World War.

The rotary press, introduced in the U.S. in 1886, could do ten times the work of the old flat bed press. It made mass-market magazines possible, and paved the way for the modern consumer magazine. The halftone press, on the other hand, meant that original art work could be reproduced without the intermediate step of making a lithograph. Publishing costs plummeted, and circulation figures skyrocketed. In 1890, a large circulation for a U.S. magazine was over 100,000. By 1900, *Ladies' Home Journal* had a circulation of almost a million copies per issue; by 1930, the total circulation of magazines in the U.S. was over 200 million, more than a magazine per person per month.

As circulation figures grew, magazines became attractive to advertisers. Overnight, magazines as small, intellectual vehicles, stamped with the personality and editorial preferences of the editor and paid for by subscription, had all but disappeared. They were replaced by glossy, larger format publications paid for primarily by, and published largely to provide a forum for, advertisers. Quality gave way to quantity, and social, artistic and intellectual communication succumbed to profit and consumerism. The U.S. market for Edith and Queenie's work had blown wide open.

Vital to Edith's career was the fact that the evolution of Canadian magazines did not parallel the U.S. pattern. Canadian readers have never accepted consumer publications or glossy advertising to the extent that Americans have. This country has had a durable (if financially precarious) tradition of literary magazines. The revolution that wiped out the literary magazine in the U.S. worked neither so quickly nor so thoroughly in Canada.

Queenie crossing a river, Quebec, 19-teens

What this meant for Edith was that the developments that spelled disaster for many careers came together at such a time and in such a way as to launch her, at age 55, into whole new territories. Travel had long been a favourite topic of the literaries. It now became a prized feature of the glossies, too. Travel photography was suddenly in great demand in both markets, and Edith was one of the few people in a position to supply it to both. She sold to literaries in Canada after their day was done in the U.S., and she was one of the earliest photographers to publish in the U.S. consumer magazines. That she had a built-in writer to provide the words for her pictures made the team of Hayward and Watson the answer to many an editor's dream, meaning as it did one assignment instead of two, one set of negotiations instead of two, and little risk of professional or temperamental clashes.

Unfortunately, the newly affluent magazines shared none of their wealth with contributors. Photographs sold for as little as two or three dollars. Stories would become more lucrative later, but the price for photographs remained steady for most of the rest of Edith's life.

These appalling prices were made possible partly by the state of photography at the time. The "Is Photography Art?" controversy was raging, and before the 1920s, the verdict was almost always in the negative. Edith considered photography an art, her art, and had no hesitations about presenting herself as a photographic artist, but magazines tended to treat photographers as minor technicians hired on occasion to fill in blanks left by underlength copy. Edith did insist upon, and got, photo credits for her work, so that in the years when photographs usually appeared anonymously, hers almost without exception bore the acknowledgement "Photo by Edith S. Watson." When a publisher omitted her name, she always wrote a scathing letter. She was well aware that her reputation and her income depended on her name, and she wanted and needed to maintain both.

The more Edith worked, the more the quality of her work varied. One editor, turning down a submission of a dozen photographs, gave a thumbnail critique in which he said that the prints ranged from snapshots to works of art of wonderful composition and design, but that her developing was sometimes so sloppy as to render even the best photographs unusable.

With one qualification he was right. Prints that appeared to be nothing more than random snapshots, and not very interesting ones, were often raw material for what drastic cropping and enlarging rendered not only saleable but intriguing photographs. It is as if the snapshot itself, taken in a hurry, is the shorthand notation for the work.

The comments about developing were true. Edith was always careful to produce high quality negatives, a fact often commented on by the companies that bought them. She was less careful with the prints she made from those negatives. Prints not properly washed and/or fixed have spotted and shaded some of her best shots, and have left much of her work more than usually prey to the ravages of time. She developed much of her material in remote places and under primitive conditions, it's true (her most sophisticated darkroom was at Wild Acres, and even there she developed in the kitchen and at the garden pump until the 1930s when running water was installed in the house), but so did many of her contemporaries who produced extremely high quality prints. Though difficult, it could be done if the photographer took the time.

Nor was Edith attached to her equipment. She changed cameras often, even during one trip, and with the exception of one Leica that she never liked, did not work with very complicated or expensive equipment. A family story says that in the first years she preferred, if she could, to go to a location with a camera, use it, develop the shots she took, and then give away the camera and all but the best negatives. She would then buy a new camera at or en route to her next stop. Whether or not the story is true, it is consistent with what we know of Edith's temperament. And when being a travelling professional photographer meant carrying a heavy camera and dozens of 4 x 5- and 8 x 10-inch glass negatives, this was a highly practical, if expensive, technique.

The time and care she skimped in the darkroom Edith gave to subjects and composition. A romantic who began working at the high point of romantic photography, she used the techniques of the day: soft focus to make photographs look like paintings, and poses reminiscent of famous paintings, in a manner now long out of fashion.

She also evolved a more individual technique, and it is in these photographs that her talent for composition and her passion for her work and subjects become evident. In a manner ahead of her time, she was aware of the beauty in angles and asymmetry. She often waited days for clouds to be right, for light to fall the right way, or for people or animals to provide the scene she wanted. Then as now many photographers imposed their own vision to create the scenes they wanted to record. While many of Edith's photographs are posed, they are not imposed; the stances and arrangements are taken out of activity in progress and respect the integrity of that activity. Edith as photographer worked with her subjects, not on them.

Queenie was a journalist. She never considered herself an artist, and never wanted to be one. She worked quickly, though if the subject did not sufficiently interest her, sometimes not quickly enough to meet deadlines. She edited her work carefully, but rarely did any rewriting. Nor did she have the artist's need to experiment with style and form. She used her writing, rather, as a vehicle to convey her delight in the places she went and the things and people she saw, and it is in this delight that its interest lies.

The pair's most frequent customer between 1914 and 1925 was the *Canadian Magazine of*

At the CPR camp in northern Ontario, probably late 1920s. Edith (left) is holding a basic box camera. This is the only photograph that shows any of her equipment
Photographer unknown

En route to Europe, 1914

Photographer unknown (Amelia Watson?)

Politics, Science, Art and Literature. During that period it published several of Queenie's articles and almost 400 of Edith's photographs.

But the *Canadian Magazine* succumbed to commercialization in 1925, when its owners sold it to the Maclean brothers. With the immediate change in policy and format came an entirely new staff and set of freelancers. Edith and Queenie never worked for the magazine again.

There were other less frequent but steady markets. During the war, both women began to sell to several large Canadian and American newspapers, in addition to the sales they had long been making to Bermudian newspapers and local papers in Newfoundland, Nova Scotia, on Cape Cod and in the Hartford area. Religious and educational publishers, particularly Ginn & Co., the Manitoba Board of Education and the Catholic and Methodist churches of both countries bought many photographs.

The National Geographic Society and the Government of Newfoundland bought hundreds of photos, as did, from the late 1890s until the mid-1920s, the CPR, CNR, and Dominion Atlantic Railway, the Plymouth Cordage and Columbian Rope companies, the Cunard Line and the Bermudiana Hotel. These customers would frequently request to see several hundred prints from which they would make a selection at a price agreed upon in advance. While many of the photographs simply disappeared into files or were used for a few months in publicity cam-

paigns, and thus did little to enhance Edith's reputation, the accounts were easy to service and provided a predictable income. Ironically, hundreds of the photographs subsequently found their way into provincial or company archives anonymously.

In June of 1914, Edith and Queenie set sail for Europe. In August they were back, the trip cut short by the outbreak of war. The return trip was made on a barge bound from England to Canada to pick up lumber, since all available ships had been commandeered for the war effort.

The war restricted travel at a time when Edith and Queenie were best financially able to explore new places. At least once, Queenie had an article cancelled because of events: it was to have run the day after Wilson severed diplomatic relations with Germany. And all publishing suffered from the paper shortage of 1917-18.

In many ways, however, the war provided Edith and Queenie with expanded prospects, much as it did for other women. The impossibility of European travel meant that they turned to further points in their own hemisphere. Edith had been to Cuba several times before she met Queenie. They now returned there together. Edith's fascination with Havana harbour and with Cuban architecture provided a whole new dimension for her work. There and in Mexico, too, she photographed marketplaces as well; these prints show the style she used in Canadian photographs applied to very different cultures. Edith had been alone several times to Nassau. Now her complimentary ticket in exchange for photographs became two tickets in exchange for photographs and articles.

In 1915 Kodak asked Edith to provide the photographs for the company's display at the Panama Exhibition. She sent 57 Canadian prints to Rochester for shipment. When she received word that Kodak was pleased and everything was ready for the display, she mounted a second set to show at the Wood Memorial Library in East Windsor Hill during the Exhibition and afterwards in Hartford. While she was travelling, word came that Kodak had changed their display, and that her work was to be dropped in order for the company to announce its latest technical advancement: easy-to-use colour film. What had promised to be the most important show of her life was reduced to a display of might-have-beens in the local library. The shock was not lessened by the suspicion that the company must have had this plan all along, and that her work was a stop-gap in case the film was not ready in time. Although the show received wildly enthusiastic reviews and was tremendously popular, nothing could compensate for Edith's disappointment.

The Canadian travels continued uninterrupted. Ste. Anne-de-Beaupré had become the base from which Edith and Queenie, and frequently Amelia, set out and to which they returned. Edith's former classmate Ellen Moore had moved there. Among the friends they made was the religious woodcarver Jobin. He became a favourite subject of

both women; most extant photographs of him at work are Edith's.

Also during these years, Edith and Queenie spent a great deal of time at West Bay, a tiny harbour outside Parrsboro, Nova Scotia. During the war many ships that had long since ceased functioning as working vessels were brought back into service to transport Canadian deal to Britain. Some of these were old wooden sailing ships, and some of those ships had figureheads. Edith had long been fascinated by figureheads and had gathered an extensive collection of photographs from northern Newfoundland to New York Harbor. This gathering of ships was a wonderful opportunity to expand the collection. The photographs were easy enough to get: hire a little boy to spend the day rowing around the harbour, holding the boat still while Edith stood to get shots and manoeuvring to get the right angles, and sometimes stopping aside the ships while Edith got permission to board and climb out onto the rigging to get shots from above.

The days not spent in the harbour were passed investigating the history of figureheads and the people who made them. Though they were fast disappearing by the beginning of this century, some of the woodcarvers who had created them were still alive and practising, and Edith and Queenie went looking for them. The result was a carton full of pictures and notes and dozens of articles.

Travel to the prairies and British Columbia increased now, too. Edith and Queenie were interested in the immigrant communities of the

Queenie (holding a camera?) looking at one of Jobin's statues, St. Pierre, c. 1918

Queenie on holiday at Hog Island, Nassau, 1916

prairies, particularly the Mennonites of Manitoba and the Doukhobors in Saskatchewan, Alberta and B.C. They spent long periods among the Mennonites; it would be the end of the war before they received permission to visit with the Doukhobors. They also visited Natives in Manitoba and the Queen Charlotte Islands, and stayed in railroad camps in northern Ontario and Manitoba, as well as visiting Banff and Lake Louise (these on assignment for the CPR).

Bermudian friends lived in Victoria, in a house on the water where Natives still came in canoes to trade. In other cities and towns Edith and Queenie boarded with families; when no housing was available, they lived in a tent and cooked at campfires. Edith did her developing in streams at night or in darkened kitchens. Equipment was simpler now, the camera usually a small Kodak, but there were still temperamental chemicals to transport as well as paper and racks for drying.

In 1918, after a lengthy correspondence with Peter Verigin and other leaders, permission came to visit the Doukhobors in their communes. Edith and Queenie spent much of the next three summers with them. They shared the Doukhobor way of life, and Edith recorded that life, from domestic chores to religious ceremonies, in a way no other outsider has ever done.

This was the height of the Doukhobor fortunes in Canada. There had been one forced removal from a settlement, the result of a dispute over rich land. They now felt safe: their remaining land was nothing anyone could covet. The struggle between Doukhobor pacifism and isolationism and Canadian federal policies had yet to escalate to the degree that would finally destroy the gentle Doukhobor way of life and the morale of the people. On the contrary, the people Edith and Queenie met were managing to wrench a more than satisfactory living from the rocky, hilly soil they had been granted.

The communes of 75 people each were prosperous. The Doukhobors lived according to their nonviolent principles, and were as content as people in unwilling exile can be. Edith's photographs constitute both a memorial to their spirit and a damnation of persecution to follow.

War's end signalled a renewed boom for publishing. Paper was no longer scarce, and much had gone unwritten and unread during the war years. Many of Edith's best customers, established magazines like *Century*, had folded during the war, but her work was appearing regularly in many others. The *Canadian Magazine*, though her best customer, was just one in a long list that included *Everywoman*, *The Canadian Courier*, *The Family Herald*, *Grain Grower's Guide*, *Canadian Home Journal*, *Maclean's*, *Saturday Night* and *Chatelaine*, and the American *National Geographic*, *Travel*, *Delineator*, *The Cunarder*, *Outing*, *Yachting*, *Rudder*, *Touchstone*, *Outlook*, *Asia*, *Town and Country*, *Arts and Decoration*, *McCall's*, *Vogue*, and even such unlikely publications as *Hygeia*, the magazine of the American Medical Association. The workload was immense: for every photograph published sometimes a dozen were submitted. *National Geographic* looked at almost a thousand, bought 300, and eventually published six.

Edith's work with newspapers grew steadily after the war. The market proved to be a mixed blessing. For the artist, newspapers proved frustrating, since the conditions of sale meant that she did not control the context in which her work appeared. Pay was poor, too. As late as 1928, the *Toronto Star* was paying $2.75 each for photographs. That year the *Detroit Free Press* paid $10.00 for two articles and their accompanying photographs. Nor did prominence of place or prestige influence prices much. The *Montreal Star* paid $8.00 for a four-photograph weekend magazine cover design, while the *New York Times Pictorial Review* bought a feature article and photographs for $18.00.

On the other hand, although this market paid no better per photograph than magazines, repeated use of one photograph, especially after she had joined the King, New York Times, Detroit Free Press and Toronto Star syndicates in the mid-1920s, meant a great deal more income and less work per photograph. The *Hartford Times* reprinted a story Edith and Queenie did about Vancouver in the First World War which appeared in the *Vancouver Sun* at the end of 1917. The *Springfield Republican* then bought the photographs, and the *New York Times* took both story and pictures. From there, they were picked up by the *Toronto Star*. Similarly, several magazines, including *Maclean's* and *Saturday Night*, printed parts of Queenie's Doukhobor article which originally appeared in the *Canadian Magazine*. After its appearance in *Romantic Canada*, the piece was reprinted by the *Montreal Star*, the *Hartford Courant*, the *New York Times* and the *Vancouver Sun*.

Ironically for someone so concerned with preserving her name in photographic art history, Edith missed out on being published by the very publications that could have done most to accomplish just that, magazines like the *Bulletin of Photography*, *The Camera* and *Photo-Era*. All of them wanted to publish her material and conducted long correspondences with her about it. But none of them paid for submissions, and Edith always insisted on being paid. She wouldn't budge on the issue, neither would they, and in the end she did herself much more harm than good by sticking to her professional standards.

This post-war phase of Edith's career was not a time of unblemished success. Men back from the war were taking jobs women had long held — in magazine publishing this included positions as freelancers and staff writers, artists and editors. The competition was keenly felt by anyone who, like Edith, was over 60 and completely financially dependent on her work. Not only that, but travel was becoming more expensive. In 1919 the CPR cancelled its policy of exchanging passes for work, a major blow to Edith's budget. Other railroads followed suit in the next couple of years. So did the ferries and the Cunard Line. For the first time, Edith and Queenie had to buy the tickets to do the travelling that earned them their living.

Fortunately, the pair had a huge reservoir of work to draw on. It is not surprising that they decided to pull some of it together into a book. (What might surprise them is that Queenie's phrase "the Canadian mosaic," which she originated in *Romantic Canada*, would find a prominent and apparently permanent place in the language, politics, culture and literature of the country.) In a tiny notebook, Queenie wrote, "Our Book. I begin work on it. Nov. 12, 1920."

They spent the spring of 1921 gathering material and formulating the concept of the book in correspondence with Hugh Eayrs, president of Macmillan Canada, and his assistant, the poet Nora Holland. The book was to be the gem of Macmillan's 1921 fall list.

The writing and photography went well. Production turned into a nightmare. Eayrs had known that extra time would be needed to allow for

On the Richelieu at Yamaska, Quebec (ESW)

difficulties with new techniques unfamiliar to even the best printers. What he didn't allow time for was a printers' strike in Toronto, Montreal and Winnipeg: every city in the country with the equipment and workers capable of producing the book. Books for the Christmas season usually appear by October. *Romantic Canada*, although it had had much advance publicity and was eagerly awaited, came off the presses on December 22. Eayrs stayed up all that night packing bookstore orders, and spent the next day delivering them. He had notified reviewers all over the continent and in Bermuda and England; they too were waiting and began their hundreds of enthusiastic reviews the minute the book arrived. But with *Romantic Canada* hitting the stands two shopping days before Christmas in Toronto, and after Christmas everywhere else, with reviews starting during the Christmas week and straggling into February, it was all too late. Everyone agreed that the book was a triumph. Sales were a disaster.

In the mid-1920s, Edith and Eayrs discussed three more book possibilities. Negotiations were long, complex, cordial and in the end, frustrating.

The first of the books was one similar to the Canada book, this time about Bermuda. Macmillan Canada, still smarting from the first book, didn't want to take the entire financial gamble. The New York branch was willing to provide moral support and distribution, but London couldn't be persuaded to make any kind of commitment, so the project was shelved for a time.

The second idea was for a book about the islands of Canada. Edith and Queenie's love affair with water had taken them to every island of the Dominion many times over by then. The book would have included them all, as well as Newfoundland, eerie Anticosti, home of pirates and shipwrecks, and St. Pierre and Miquelon. A more personal narrative than that in *Romantic Canada*, it would give the flavour of each island, a bit of geography and history, and profiles of the people.

Eayrs loved the idea, but was cautious: he wasn't sure the time was right, and wondered about the book's marketability in Canada. He thought the British would find such a book exotic, that perhaps the English office might produce it if they were guaranteed distribution assistance in Canada, the U.S., Bermuda and France. London had little to say about his proposals, and the project dropped from sight.

Negotiations for *Romantic Bermuda*, however, began to look more promising. The English office decided that Eayrs should work with Edith and Queenie since they had worked well together before, and since they met regularly: when Edith and Queenie couldn't be in Toronto, they were within a day's reach by mail, and Eayrs and his wife frequently visited Bermuda when the pair were there. That none of this travel was at Macmillan's expense increased the appeal of the plan. London also reached an agreement with New York whereby both offices would buy outright several hundred copies of the book from the Toronto branch, thereby reducing the risks it took.

The third scheme involved pulling together 30 years' worth of notes and photographs into a book of figureheads from 1870 to 1920 and from northern Newfoundland to New York.

By the time Edith suggested this book, Eayrs was almost certain of success with *Romantic Bermuda*. If he could get the Bermuda government to buy a hundred copies, and if Edith and Queenie would agree to buy a large number of copies themselves, it would be time to sign a contract. It was an unusual, but workable, compromise.

Edith and Queenie agreed to buy a hundred copies. The Bermuda government agreed to buy a hundred copies. The contract was drawn up and signed.

And then, for reasons that remain obscure, the Bermuda government backed out. *Romantic Bermuda* fell through. A few days later, Eayrs wrote to Edith that the figurehead book was impossible. Edith and Queenie's career in book publishing was over. The notes and photographs for the figurehead book, the notes for the island book, and the signed contract and Queenie's completed manuscript for *Romantic Bermuda* went into an attic trunk.

By the end of the 1920s money was extremely tight. The U.S. mania for travel had faded, and with it much of the market for Edith's kind of work. The *Canadian Magazine* was gone, which drastically cut Edith's exposure to Canadians. *Romantic Canada* was no source of income, and the other books never would be. The sisters had rented out the cottage at Martha's Vineyard for

A happy day at St. Pierre and Miquelon (ESW), 19-teens. Queenie is in the middle

Queenie writing on the pier at Percé, 19-teens

a week or two each summer since the early '20s. They now started to rent it for all of July and August. Amelia sold some family land in Tennessee at a tremendous loss; she and Edith both sold inherited railroad stock, also at a frightening loss. Family jewelry went too. In 1930 Amelia had to sell her house in Tryon. The next year she received relief payments for several months. Edith was 69, Amelia five years older, and the Great Depression had just begun.

Colour photography was by this time available to amateurs; it would not be accepted into art photography for another thirty years. The interim step, nurtured by the urge to make photographs more like both nature and painting, and believed to combine the best features of both, was the hand-painted photograph. Although bizarre to modern eyes, with their often rather garish colours over the metallic gloss of a photograph, these photographs were immensely popular for 40 years. Edith and Amelia had started to produce them before the First World War. They now became the backbone of the sisters' income.

Amelia provided much of the painting, while Edith supplied the photographs, some of the painting, and the business negotiations. They split income after expenses. Amelia kept track of mutual expenses, such as taxes on the house, and billed Edith for her share. All personal expenses remained separate down to their accounts with the milkman. It was very much a day-to-day existence; Millie's diary contains many entries like this one:

"Letter from Edie with check for $9.00. Thank God." The amounts Edith sent home seldom reached more than $20 at any one time, and were sometimes as little as $1.

Ironically it was during this hardest time that both Edith and Amelia spent extended periods in Europe. In 1929 Edith went, paid for by her life-long friend, Libby Jerome. "Dearest love," Amelia wrote in a note delivered to Edith's cabin aboard ship, "I trust this finds you all cozily ensconced in your stateroom … 'Baby Edith', going forth with the magic camera once more … Love and blessings, from Sister Minnie."

The next year Amelia spent four months in an orgy of French, Italian and English art galleries and museums. That the trip was entirely paid for, and the itinerary dictated, by her cousin Grace Wilson, bothered Amelia not at all. She had a glorious time and left a diary/scrapbook full of postcards and sketches that was still unfinished at her death.

After Amelia lost the Tryon house, she spent winters in Florida with Grace and the Beach cousins. Two days after Christmas in 1933 she boarded a bus for Orlando, where she had arranged a gallery show for January. On her way to the gallery on the 28th she had a heart attack and died on the street.

Edith wrote obituaries for a dozen newspapers, organized Millie's things and gave paintings and her collection of Chinese teapots to various people, museums and libraries. Amelia had been systematically destroying her private letters for years, none remain. Edith kept her diaries and scrapbooks. The care she put into ordering Millie's things and distributing her more than 500 bequests provides ample record of Edith's devotion to her sister.

Although she and Queenie spent less time at Wild Acres after Amelia's death, they are well remembered. Some neighbours found Edith standoffish, others speak warmly of her. She and Queenie were certainly a familiar sight as they made their daily quarter-mile walk to the post office, Queenie always the cordial lady, Edith brisk and somewhat mannish in dress and manner.

In 1937 Edith and Queenie went to Europe together. They started in Paris, then wandered through the south of France and into Italy, from there swinging north through Switzerland and Germany, then to Le Havre for the ship home. There are snapshots of the two of them at the ship's dining table, long lists of the cities they visited, and whenever possible, a map of the town with an X and an arrow: "Our room," "We stayed here," "Our view of the Seine." It was a perfect expedition for two romantic old ladies who had spent their lives exploring.

Edith and Queenie never fully retired, but life proceeded at a much easier pace. They continued to sell photographs and to travel. They, too, now spent winters in Florida, and they fed Edith's incessant need to be on the go by numerous wanderings in New England. And their income improved, making the last years comfortable ones.

Edith's wanderlust made it difficult to get her to stay in any one place for long, and despite her own love of travel, Queenie found herself packing and moving more frequently than she liked. She particularly enjoyed time spent at Martha's Vineyard, where life consisted, in addition to many movies and visits with friends around the island, pretty much of the kinds of domesticity sandwiched in Queenie's diaries between news of the horrors of Hitler's invasion of Poland and the submarine war in the Atlantic:

Monday [August 26, 1939]

E. scared stiff from morning to night with all the talk about War and Hitler. Now up now down. Drat the man! I have given up reading newspapers and do all I can to keep Edith pried from the subject. "Rumours of War" are frightening things I trust they may never be confirmed, but Edith chews upon every newssheet and emphasises every horror until I feel as if I had been in the thick of the fight that doesn't exist.

Thursday morning August 29, 1939

No war yet! Can hire a rowboat I am told for 25cts an hour. 3 little girls in trousers and jerseys and a little boy going off in a boat. Bailing out at present. I must have looked as they do, except I had no comfortable trousers only half wet skirts. In many things this is a more sensible age. Little girls in blue trousers lose none of the attractiveness of feminine youth.

Friday

Go in the morning to see the exhibition of water colors and oil paintings. Really very good. Paid 10 cents entrance. Each entitled to vote on the pictures, the one getting the most votes gets one hundred dollars. Edith voted for a picture by Polly Nordell, and I voted for one by Harry de Maine, both very well painted we thought. Coming away in the yard we met Miss Nordell who invited us to go up to her studio, we accepted and spent a most delightful time looking at her pictures.

And she a real charmer! Had just come back from Quebec. Had a number of very good sketches from there, many of places we knew intimately. But her flower paintings were really wonderful. All framed, had just come back from some exhibition. She had studied in Paris. Writes poetry a little to fit some of her pictures. Had a great many press notices. Teaches here and in Boston. Very much of a lady and undoubtedly has a brilliant mind.

Saturday

The beach crowded with little human sandflippers, meaning children, but many leaving. We did not stay, walked up the hill road and down the other side and came to coast of rocks and rolling surf. It was still very hot but Edith enchanted, elected to stay at that spot. I went on to a point which made out further to sea and caught the breeze so I sat down on the granite rocks in as soft a place as I could find and there arranged thus, we sat for hours. Nothing like the surf of the ocean to tear the cobwebs out of one's brain. I suppose Polly Nordell would have written a poem on what we watched and felt but not us. That's the difference between poetry and prose. I do not know how a poetess would have got home but E and I took to "shank's mare" and for every step taken the road seemed to stretch out like gutta percha. Edith arrived thoroughly impressed by the great length of the road.

And in the mood I had entertained on the outward way. No doubt there's something strikes a balance. Thus do we two suit each other to a T. E took out her viciousness on the preparation of a good tea. Boiled corn on the cob, cold ham, shredded wheat biscuit, milk, cinnamon buns, bananas, peaches, tomatoes. I hope she will get "mad" with another road. All I produced was an appetite.

Monday, Labor Day, September 4th, 1939

The 8:15 train to Boston. Horrified … to find newspaper with the headlines of the submarining of S.S. Att with 1400 passengers. What an inhuman act! Can't believe that our race contains such barbarians in this enlightened age. But there it is.

Ye who will may take coast resorts, but for me, I want an island. Where the wind blows wild and free all around it. Now if Hitler had only been born on an island! but he may end up on one à la Napoleon.

We boarded the steamer for the Island at Wood's Hole and half an hour later were at Oak Bluffs. We walked around the harbor and took possession of our dear cottage on the Highlands of East Chop.

Saturday Sept. 9th

The summer folks all gone home so we had all this beauty of the world to ourselves. Wonderful! And all the way by the shore road was sprinkled by broken sea shells, mostly clams, sprinkled there by the clever seagulls who get a clam and then fly high and drop it breaking it as it hits the hard road below. Talk about marvels. I think this trick of seabirds one of the smartest I ever heard of employed by wild animals to feed themselves. In Oak Bluffs we got a loaf of delicious homemade oatmeal bread, some home-baked beans, some small cakes and three raspberry turnovers, delicious … Not very cheap, three for 10 cents.

Monday Sept. 11th 1939

Edith out-of-doors waging war on the green moss coming up in the grass. She does not like indoor work. But she cooks breakfast always. I have attacked the oil stove, and ascertained why it flickers. The drum has rusted at the top. So it has a good excuse for behaving thus.

Played Backgammon as usual last night. Unusually good games and very close.

Wednesday

E. has indigestion & is she not cross? Nothing I can do suits her. I wonder, I wonder. I sit in the yellow rocker in the grassy backyard. A blue jay arrives. E. sits on the kitchen steps refuses the chair I proffer. Very disgruntled.

Thursday

How glorious a morning it is! Have basked in the sun. Tropical and wine-y. This is the time of the year to truly enjoy this island I find, and it's what the Vineyarders themselves say. But for one reason or another most of the summer people leave here in a rush the minute Labor Day is over amounting to a wholesale Exodus. I sincerely wish that the American people could learn to relax. No need for the whole family to end their holiday because a child or two has to attend an opening school. A good six weeks is still to be enjoyed in the plein air before snow. Surely satisfactory arrangements could be made for the children if parents were master of the situation. The children too could come back for the weekends. La, La no one so headstrong and difficult as parents. Eh, children?

Tuesday Sept. 19th

The news yesterday from the Eastern front said "Poland overrun by Nazis and the Soviets." Poor Poland! No telling what's ahead for the whole world.

Edith's chronic indigestion, and with it her temperament, grew increasingly worrisome. On December 14, 1943, she and Queenie left Wild Acres for St. Petersburg. The six-and-a-half-day journey exhausted Edith. She died in hospital after abdominal surgery 36 hours after their arrival in Florida. Queenie wrote:

Wednesday December 22

Oh my dear. My dear, dear Edith.

The doctor came in to look at her, he said it is a large ulcer burst there was a hole as big as that, as he joined his forefinger and thumb together. The sister told me "You were lucky not to have her die on you on the bus — on the way here." O my dear. I'm sitting on the side of my bed at the hotel writing waiting for daylight to come & my heart is bursting. Oh my dear — we've been together 30 years. She had a special nurse, the Dr. said to have one & sister asked if I could afford it, yes of course certainly I want her to have one … she came at once — my dear Edith did not require her services long. — Wed. 3:00 a.m.

Subsequent diaries chronicle the extent of Queenie's loss, the loneliness and courage of her life without Edith. Perhaps most poignant is this entry from August 24, 1944:

My dear, sweet Edith! … I will try to do the best I can, — words fail me to say how much I love you and how I miss you, how I wish you could have lived to enjoy it all — I feel very sad tonight knowing how hard you worked and you not here to enjoy it. I have expressed it very poorly I know but my heart is about broken never to see her or hear her voice.

Edith was buried in the cemetery that is a ten-minute walk from Wild Acres. Queenie wrote of her tombstone:

It looks very nice and just like the others, her father's and mother's, and Minnie's, which was what she wished. A rabbit ran away from eating the grass on her grave as I came near. She would have liked that touch.

Edith's tombstone is not quite exactly like those of her parents and sister. In addition to her name and dates is the inscription,

They seek a country.

Queenie fishing at Percé, 19-teens

Photographs

These photos are taken from Edith's personal albums, which she kept at Wild Acres and which remained there after her death. There is one album of her travels to Canada and elsewhere with Queenie, one of Canadian travels with Queenie, and fourteen albums of her Canadian wanderings. Most of the albums are the cheap 12 1/2 x 14 1/2 -inch scrapbooks available at any five and dime or stationery store during much of this century. Edith has given some of these books general titles, such as *Children from Here and There* or *The Way of Wells, Pots and Ovens*; they portray one subject in many places. Others are geographically or ethnically specific: *Ste. Anne* is one of these, *Galicians, Hungarians, Mennonites, and Indians in the Canadian West* another, *A Souvenir of Alert Bay, B.C. and the West Coast to the border of Alaska and The Queen Charlotte Is. and the Haida Indian Reservation at Old Massett* another. A few combine place and subject, as in *A Story of Fish in Newfoundland, Nova Scotia, St. Pierre, Percé, etc.*, and a couple of titles, notably *Happy Souvenirs of trips made alone to Newfoundland and to Labrador in the company of Miss Victoria Hayward, the Writer,* hint at place and date. Trips made alone to Newfoundland, for example, would have been before 1912, those with "Miss Victoria Hayward, the Writer," after that time.

Many of the photographs are difficult to date. Edith's wanderings did follow an east to west, earlier to later pattern. Thus, there are no images of British Columbia before at least the late 19-teens, and most of the Newfoundland photos seem to have been taken between 1894 and 1910. One is dated September 1902. From her earliest travels, however, Edith went through Nova Scotia. She produced photographs for a 1906 travel brochure for the Nova Scotia government. She and Queenie also spent much time in the province during the First World War. Thus, photographs of Halifax may be earlier, and some show buildings destroyed in the Halifax Explosion. Others, such as those in West Bay and Parrsboro, are probably, whether so marked or not, from 1915, '16 or '17. After prolonged correspondence with Peter Verigin, Edith and Queenie spent the summers of 1918, '19 and '20 with the Doukhobors. It is unlikely that they also went to the east coast during those times.

If we knew more about the technical aspects of Edith's work, that information might help clarify times and dates. Although several hundred of the albumen prints she developed and kept remain in these albums (as well as three other albums that have recently surfaced, two in the National Archives and one at the Notman Archives, and I suspect several hundred more single or collected prints that are scattered around Canada, the U.S. and Bermuda), all but twelve of her 8 x 10-inch glass plate negatives have been lost. Those that still exist are of very early Newfoundland scenes: mostly the geese in the Petries' yard. With one very important rider, it appears that she may have used more complex equipment in her early work, opting for simpler cameras later. However, she negotiated so much equipment with camera companies that they sometimes ran out or were unable to provide more than a certain amount of any one thing, making it necessary to use what they were willing to supply, so it is difficult to estimate what materials she was using at any specific time.

Every life is and remains a mystery; that is at least part of why we humans so fascinate each other. Edith's story challenges many of our assumptions. The images she made give us glimpses into the lives of the people and groups who made up most of Canada at the turn of the century. Together, her life and images will, if we let them, broaden our horizons and deepen our understanding. The miracle here is that the greater the revelation, the greater the mystery.

All photographs are by Edith S. Watson. The initials "ESW" with a caption indicate that the caption is Edith's own, as it appears with the photograph in her personal album. The phrase "photo back" indicates Edith's or Queenie's written notes on the back of the album photograph. Each photograph has been scanned and digitally processed without additional manipulation so as to preserve its original character, including flaws, as faithfully as possible.

The homemade pieced bed quilt often comes in handy for bringing in the hay in the Nfld outports where horses are unknown. In Hermitage (ESW)

Harvesting Hay, Hermitage (ESW)
Caption on another photo – The women and
children harvest the hay while the men of the
family are away at the fishing. Horses are
unknown in many of these outports of
Newfoundland

Spruce boughs for firewood. Hermitage, Nfld. (ESW)

photo back — Spreading fish, Burgeo, Nfld.

Burgeo — *At the well (ESW)*

Carrying water from the public well, Burgeo Nfld. (ESW)
Caption from another photo — In Nfld, the hoop holds
the bucket out and keeps the water from spilling.

Here in Burgeo the public well serves the whole
community. No water is drawn on Sunday!

Uncle Tom and Lovey on board the schooner Hilton,
from Nippers Harbor to the French shore at La Scie, Aug
22nd [1902] (ESW)

photo back — Tom [Borland] and Lovey, Nippers Har. en route
to Scie Cove from Nippers Harbor. Another photograph notes
that Edith boarded with Lovey, apparently over several years.

Capt Borland on board "The Stellata" [?]
off Penguin Head, bound for the Goose
Arm. Sep. 8, 1902. (ESW)
Typed note on photo back — Where Time
Stands Still, March Outing, 1915

A typical outport. Nippers Harbor, Notre Dame Bay, Nfld. (ESW)

Fish Stages, Quidi Vidi, Nfld. (ESW), c. 1900

Dismantling the great whale, Snookes Arm. A work that always fetches an audience if carried out ashore! (ESW)

Mrs. Petrie feeding the flock in the lane at "Petrie's Point," Bay of Islands, Nfld. (ESW)

In Hopedale, Moravian Mission, Labrador (ESW)

Photo back, in Queenie's handwriting —
A Nova Scotia boy extracting bones, with a pair of
tweezers, for boneless codfish. In Sambro, c. World War I

Beheading codfish, Sambro (ESW)

Fisherman's luck! Peggy's Cove, Nova Scotia (ESW)

Packing Mackerel, Halifax, Nova Scotia (ESW)

Codfish drying on the house tops, Halifax, Nova Scotia (ESW)

photo back — The "Tonu" (Norwegian) (ESW)
Then, in Queenie's handwriting — "The British
Lion." Below that, again in ESW's writing — by
John Rogerson. Halifax

photo back — The Lalla Rookh, W. Bay, N.S. Carved by John Rogerson, St. John. N.B.

Typed note with photo — THE LALLAH ROOKH. An Englisd (sic) Barque, built in England, in 1876. The very beautiful Figurehead was carved by John Rogerson, A Master Carver, of St. John, N.B. The figure all in white. Her head turned, and looking out to sea. Frank T. Bullen, the novelist, served apprentice as a sailor on the LALLAH ROOKH, and was second mate for awhile. Author of "CHRIST AT SEA." The ship was sold to the Norwegians. Photo was taken at West Bay, near Parrsboro, N.S. in the fall of 1915

The business of digging clams for bait during mackerel season is entirely a low tide industry. It employs most of the women and children in the Magdalens. At Le Bassin, Amherst Island (ESW)

On the boys' side. In an Acadian school. La Meque, Shippegan Is.,
N.B. (ESW)

Mama makes the baby's cap, and papa makes her
"go-cart" in St. Pierre et Miquelon (ESW)

Homeward bound, St. Joachim, Quebec (ESW),
early 19-teens

Little "Marie" in her improvised bateau. Cap Tormente, Que. (ESW)

The first strawberries in the convent garden. Sisters of the order of Ste. Rosaire (ESW). Ste. Anne-de-Beaupré

To Louis Jobin.

Louis Jobin, Canada's famous carver of religious figures,
figureheads, etc., in his shop in Ste. Anne-de-Beaupré (ESW)

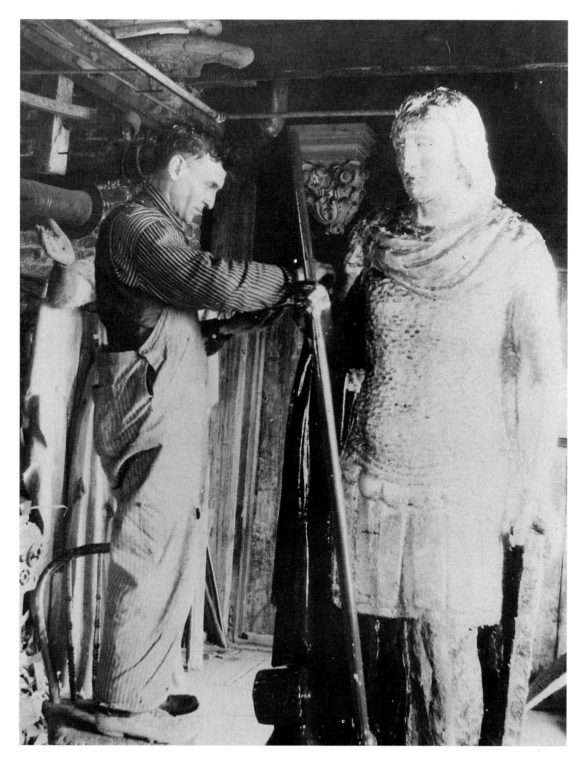

M. Louis Jobin has only one shop man, his nephew, who assists him in the delicate work of laying on the gold leaf to some of his statues (ESW)

At Nicolet, convent school (ESW)

Dog carts and dinner pails! (ESW)

Harvesting sweetgrass, Pierreville, Quebec (ESW)
Although Edith mentions two places, this and the facing
photograph clearly show the same woman.

Harvesting sweetgrass for the basket industry among the
Abenaki Indians at Odonak (ESW)

The ferry landing at Pierreville on the Richelieu River,
opposite St. François-du-Lac (ESW)

The ferry landing at Yamaska (ESW)

Treading out oats in the good old way (ESW)

photo back — Threshing out oats. Yamaska, P.Q.

Ann Grogan on old Champlain Is. Que. (ESW)

*photo back in Edith's handwriting — On Gordon Pew [?] schooner
collecting fish. Percé, Quebec. In Queenie's handwriting — Photograph of
Victoria Hayward in conference with the cook. What's for dinner?
(early 19-teens)*

The Hotel Frontenac, the old town below. From the

Dufferin Terrace (ESW)

Our guide drinking off his paddle, Crooked Lake,
Ont. (ESW)

photo back — At French River camp bound for Crooked

Lake, Ont. (ESW)

At the Indian Reservation, Brantford Ont. (ESW)

photo back — In the cucumber patch. Kildonan truck farm near Winnipeg, Man.

Bunching up rhubarb for market on a Kildonan truck farm (ESW)

Harvesting and sorting Italian onions for the pickle factories of Winnipeg, Manitoba (ESW)

photo back – Kildonan truck farm. Caption on another photograph – The seeds for these clean, silvery onions are annually imported from Italy. Winnipeg is a city of many pickle factories which obtain their vegetables from the farms along the Red River.

A Galician from the old country. Gonor, Manitoba
(ESW)

A Galician woman in an inverted sheepskin coat, brought from the old country, in the doorway of her prairie farm in Gonor, Man. (ESW)

A Bulcominian [?] learned all about
mushrooms and how to cook them in the
old country. In Gonor, Man. (ESW)

Cree babies, tucked away in their gay-colored
"tikinagans." At the Pas, Manitoba (ESW)

An Indian woman drying fox skins at the Pas, Canada (ESW)

photo back – Drying skins (moose and fox)

In the Mennonite village of Osterick, Manitoba (ESW)

*The village herd luxuriates at mid-day in a long drink
and dip. Osterick, Mtba. (ESW)*

A "stooker" all the way from Scotland, Pine Bluff, Man. (ESW)
photo back — Scotch man for the Prairie [illeg.] at High Bluff,
Man. On prairie farm

Our hospitable hostess at Otthon, peeling mushrooms, which grow wild
here in the fields (ESW)
photo back — Our landlady where we stayed

A group of Hungarian social service workers, New Stockholm, Sask. Sister Slochta, second from left (ESW) Note with another photo – Sister Margaret Slochta from Budapest, in Hungary, on a visit to the Hungarian "Sisters of Social Service" in Stockholm, Sask. She is often spoken of as "Hungary's most famous woman," the first woman to be selected a Member of the Hungarian Parliament

photo back — Lake Louise

Mount Edith, Road to Sun Dance Canyon. Banff (ESW)

On the road to Sun Dance Canyon, after the rain (ESW)

Not bits of statuary, but live Rocky Mountain goats, in the Rocky Mountain Park, at Banff. Lake Louise (ESW)

An incomplete set
of Doukhobor pictures.

A souvenir of three or
more delightful visits, among
these most kindly & hospitable
people, in Brilliant and
Grand Forks. B.C and last of
all in Verigin, Sask. where
we had the good fortune to meet
and talk with Peter Verigin,
the Doukhobor leader, and of whom
I was permitted to take pictures.
Many of an illustrated articles
have appeared in well known
magazines & newspapers both here
& in Canada. A set of four
of my Doukhobor photos came
out in "Asia" magazine.
Miss Victoria Hayward, the writer
has accompanied me in my
many & varied travels.
Edith S. Watson

Mr Peter Verigin, President of the Christian Community of Universal Brotherhood, giving directions to a group of men who just arrived from one of the fruit growing communities to the prairie community at Verigin, Sask., to help in the wheat harvest (ESW)

Peacefully sleeping! Where I was asked to attend the funeral & take this photo. Verigin, Sask. (ESW)

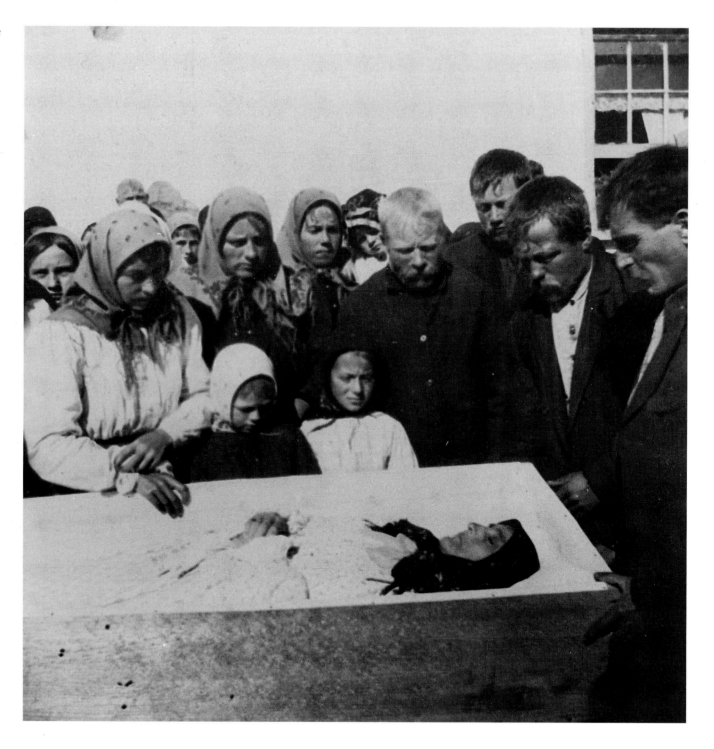

Harvest time, Grand Forks, B.C. Doukhobor Community (ESW)

photo back — Her load of beans, Brilliant, B.C.

Harvesting flax, Brilliant B.C. (ESW)

*The Doukhobor community owns a large commercial
jam factory, but each housewife likes to make her own
jam and dry her own fruit (ESW)*

An outdoor religious ceremony; women and men both
wore homemade linen clothing and no shoes for religious
observations (ESW)

Plastering a ceiling. Plaster [is made] out of dung and sand.
The plaster is applied by hand and when dry is very artistic
in color (ESW)

As the Doukhobors are vegetarians, they use a great deal of dried fruit. The fruit goes into the big oven in the [illeg.] when baked in a slow fire, goes in the sun to dry in great trays (ESW)

Queenie harvesting fruit with Doukhobor women, Brilliant, B.C.

It is not only old fingers that hold the knitting needles. Look at this baby picking up a dropped stitch! Brilliant, B.C. (ESW)

A Community Doukhobor village. In Brilliant, B.C. (ESW)

An apple paring bee, Brilliant, B.C. (ESW)

"A Madonna of the Kootenays," "Between Trains"
on the CPR near Windermere (ESW)
photo back — A Kootenay Indian, taken on the platform
of a train, near Windermere, B.C., c. 1920

Chinese celebration for the dead, lighting the [illeg.] sticks,
Victoria, B.C. (ESW)

photo back — This picture illustrates how closely the totem enters into the family life. The big tree "temple" is the framework for a giant community house. The founder of this family was the bear. Alert Bay

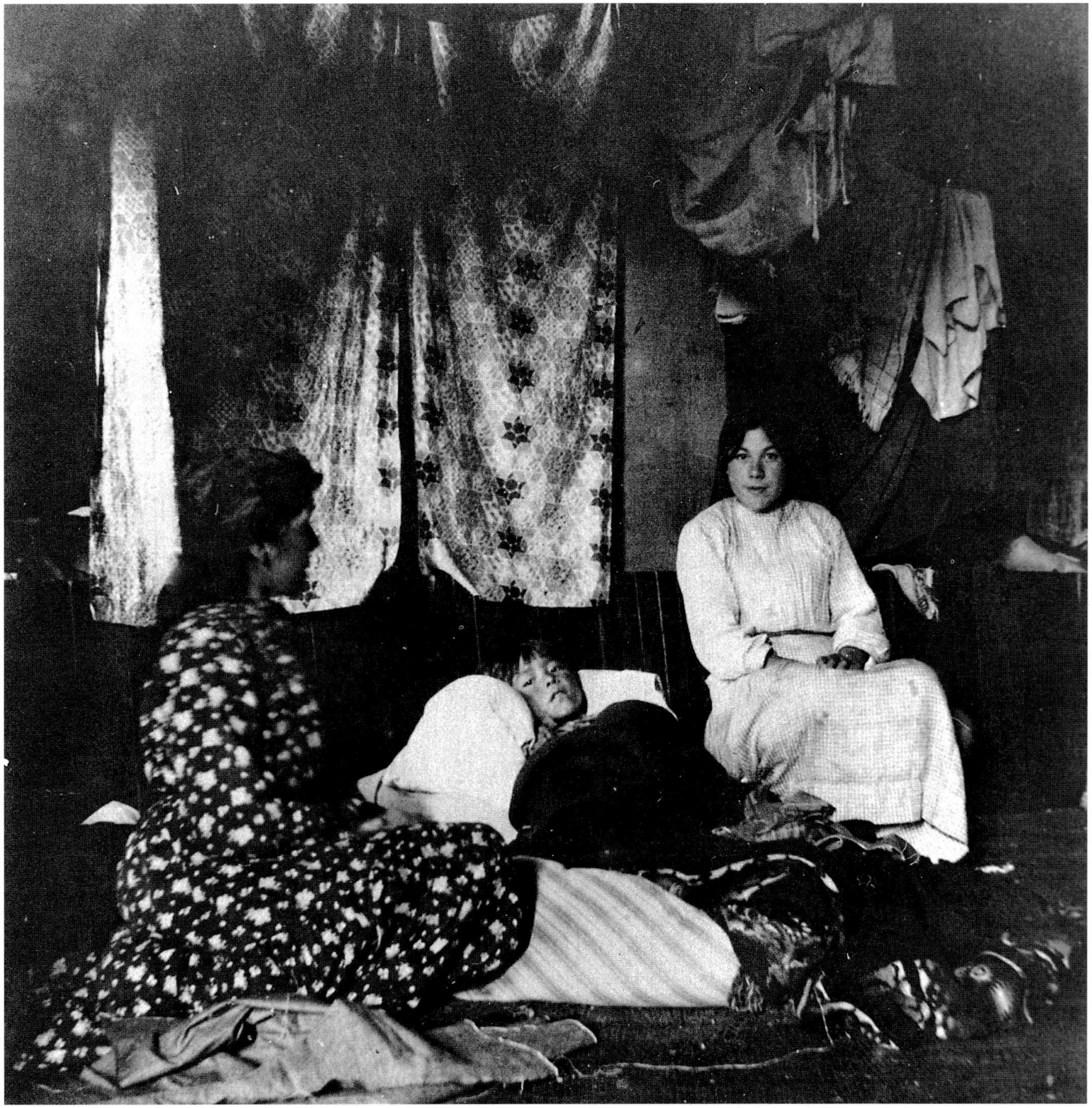

photo back – In a community house at Alert Bay

Detail from the totem pole family tree of the Siwash
Indians at Alert Bay, B.C. (ESW)

Of the Whale tribe. Graphic epitaph above the grave of
a coastal Indian in the graveyard at Alert Bay (ESW)

Native canoeing, Queen Charlotte Islands

This Haida Indian woman is 90 years old and walks six miles every day. Her son is the Chief Councillor of the Indian reservation. Old Massett, Queen Charlotte Islands, B.C. (ESW)

Horses grazing on meadowland at Stewart, on the boundary of Alaska (ESW)

Selected Bibliography

In addition to photograph albums, the Watson material includes loose photographs, hand-coloured photographs, negatives, watercolours, sketchbooks and paintings; exhibit catalogues, books ESW and AMW illustrated, pamphlets Edith illustrated; AMW and VH diaries, scrapbooks of travels; scrapbooks of reviews (beginning with *My First Scrapbook*, *1887*); lists of sales; family letters, wills, the manuscript of *Romantic Bermuda*, the *Romantic Canada* contract, publishers' letters, copies of ESW's letters to publishers, editors, photographic supply companies and other clients, and letters concerning stocks and bonds and the Tennessee property.

Magazines and newspapers referred to, in addition to those noted in the text, include *Afterimage*, 1975-82; *American Annual of Photography*, 1900-37; *American Journal of Photography; Art Journal; Blatant Image*, 1981-83; *Canadian Homes and Gardens*, 1926-28; *Country Life in America,* 1912; *Editor and Publisher*, 1926, 1936; *Family Herald* and *Weekly Star*, 1934-36; *Harper's; Photo-Era; Royal Gazette* and *Colonist* (Bermuda), 1928; *Telegram* (Quebec), 1935; *Windsor Tribune* (Nova Scotia), 1907; *World Traveller Magazine*, 1928.

"Another Mrs. Gainsborough on sale." (1983, June 11). *Toronto Star*: E27.

Bolles, Frederick. (1891). *Land of the Lingering Snow*. Boston and New York: Houghton Mifflin.

————. (1894). *From Blomidon to Smoky and Other Papers*. Boston and New York: Houghton Mifflin.

"British Columbia. Practical Advice to the Intending Settler." (1906, March). *Review of Reviews*, 33:381-82.

Brown, Robert Craig, and Ramsay Cook. (1974). *Canada 1896-1921: A Nation Transformed*. Toronto: McClelland & Stewart.

Call, F.O. (1926). *The Spell of French Canada*. Boston: L.C. Page. ESW photog. 124 opp.

Campbell, Barbara Kuhn. (1979). *The "Liberated" Woman of 1914*. Studies in American History and Culture, No. 6. Np: UMI Research Press.

Claudy, C.H. (1910, July). "The Cost of Photography as a Hobby." *Photo-Era*, 25 (1):3-12.

Coke, V.D. (1964). *The Painter and the Photograph*. Albuquerque, NM.

Cook, Blanche Wiesen. (1979, Spring/Summer). "The Historical Denial of Lesbianism." *Radical History Review,* 20:60-64.

Cook, D.E. (1870). *Sherlock Holmes and Much More or Some of the Facts about William Gillette*. Hartford: Connecticut Historical Society.

Cott, Nancy. (1977). *The Bonds of Womanhood: "Woman's Sphere" in New England, 1780-1835*. New Haven: Yale.

Daniel, Pete, and Raymond Smock. (1974). *A Talent for Detail. The Photographs of Miss Frances Benjamin Johnston, 1889-1910*. New York: Harmony.

Doty, R. (1960). *Photo-Secession: Photography as a Fine Art*. Rochester, NY: George Eastman House.

Evalenko, A.M. (1913). *The Message of the Doukhobors*. New York: International Library Publishing Co.

Faderman, Lillian. (1981). *Surpassing the Love of Men*. New York: Morrow.

Freedman, Estelle. (1974, September). "The New Woman: Changing Views of Women in the 1920's." *Journal of American History*, 61.

French, Wilfred A. (1910, October). "Women in Photography." *Photo-Era,* 4:186.

Gernsheim, H. (1962). *Creative Photography: Aesthetic Trends 1839-1960*. London and Boston.

Gilpin, Laura. (1926). "The Need for Design in Photography." *American Annual of Photography*, 154-57.

Gordon, Colin. (1978). *A Richer Dust. Echoes from an Edwardian Album*. London: Elm Tree.

Griffiths, N.E.S. (1976). *Penelope's Web*. Toronto: Oxford.

Hartford in 1912. (1912). Hartford: Hartford Post.

Hayward, Victoria, and Edith S. Watson. (1922). *Romantic Canada*. Toronto: Macmillan.

Hayward, Victoria. *Romantic Bermuda*. Unpublished ms.

Hedges, J.B. (1939). *Building the Canadian West*. New York: Historical Society.

Ingraham, P. (ed.). (1885). *Saratoga: Winter and Summer*. New York: American Bank Note Co.

Innis, H.A. (1971). *A History of the Canadian Pacific Railway*. Toronto: University of Toronto Press.

James, Edward T., Janet Wilson James, et al. (1971). *Notable American Women*, 2 vols. Cambridge: Harvard University Press.

Jones, Laura. (1983). *Rediscovery: Canadian Women Photographers, 1841-1941*. Exhibition catalogue. London: London Regional Art Gallery.

————, ed. (1986). Women Photographers. Special issue of *Canadian Woman Studies*, 7 (3).

Kelly-Gadol, Joan. (1976, Summer). "The Social Relation of the Sexes: Methodological Implications of Women's History." *Signs*, 1 (4):809-23.

Labrador Guidebook, 1911. (1911).

Lerner, Gerda. (1975, Fall). "Placing Women in History: Definitions and Challenges." *Feminist Studies*, 3 (1/2):5-14.

Longstreth, T. Morris. (1924). *The Lake Superior Country*. New York: Century.

————. (1935). *To Nova Scotia, The Sunrise Province of Canada*. New York: Appleton-Century.

Macmillan of Canada. *A Canadian Publishing House*. (1923). Toronto: Author.

McGrath, P.T. (1906, June). "What People Read in Canada." *Review of Reviews*, 33:720-22.

Marchbin, Andred. (1935). "Early Emigration from Hungary to Canada." *Slavonic Review*, 13:127-38.

Middleton, D. (l965). *Victorian Lady Travellers*. New York: E.P. Dutton.

Minden, Robert. (1979). *Separate from the World: Meetings with Doukhobor-Canadians in British Columbia*. Vancouver: National Film Board of Canada.

Morley, M.W. (1895). *Love and Life*. New York: McClury.

————. (1897). *A Few Familiar Flowers*. New York: Ginn.

————. (1897). *Flowers and their Friends*. New York: Ginn. (Inscribed: Minne Amelia Watson, With the love of the Perpetrator).

————. (1900). *Down North and Up Along*. New York: Dodd Mead. ESW photos. (Inscribed: Edith S. Watson, Interior Decorator, with love from the Perpetrator).

————. (1913). *The Carolina Mountains*. Boston: Houghton Mifflin. Frontispiece, cover ill., end-paper drawing, AMW.

Morley, M.W. (1913). *The Spark of Life. The Story of How Living Things Come into the World as told for Girls and Boys*. New York: Fleming H. Revell.

Muir, John. (1916). *A Thousand Mile Walk to the Gulf*. Boston: Houghton Mifflin. 1 sketch, AMW.

Newhall, Beaumont. (1964). *The History of Photography*. New York: Museum of Modern Art.

Novotny, Anne. (1976). *Alice's World: The Life and Photography of American Original Alice Austen, 1866-1952*. Old Greenwich, CT: Chatham Press.

Nutting, Wallace. (1923). *Massachusetts Beautiful*. Garden City: Garden City Publishing.

Oats, Robert F. (1978). "Things Fearful to Name." *Journal of Social History*, 12 (2):268-81.

"The Pas, Gateway to Hudson Bay." Booklet #1. (1914).

Peterson, Theodore. (1964). *Magazines in the Twentieth Century*. Urbana: University of Illinois.

Reunion Hartford Female Seminary, June 9, 1892. (1892). Hartford: Case, Lockwood, Brainard. (Hartford Public Library)

Rinhart, Floyd, and Marion Rinhart. (1978). *Summertime. Photographs of Americans at Play, 1850-1900*. New York: Potter.

Rooney, Frances. (1981). "Finding Edith S. Watson." *Blatant Image,* 1:86.

————. (1982). "Edith S. Watson, Photographer, and Victoria Hayward, Writer." *Fireweed,* 13:60-68.

————. (1983, March). "Finding Edith S. Watson." *Resources for Feminist Research,* 12 (1):26-28.

————. (1986, Fall). "Edith S. Watson: A Photoessay." *Canadian Woman Studies,* 7 (3): 48-49.

————. (1991). *Edith S. Watson: Rural Canadians at Work, 1890-1920.* Exhibition catalogue. Sackville, NB: Owens Art Gallery, Mount Allison University.

————. (1994). *My Dear, Dear Edith.* Exhibition catalogue. Galiano Island: Nuse Gallery.

Rothstein, A. (1979). *Photojournalism.* Alexandria, VA: Time-Life.

Rowbotham, Sheila. (1976). "Middle-Class Women Begin to Organize." In *Hidden from History.* New York: Vintage.

Ryan, Mary. (1975). *Womanhood in America: From Colonial Times to the Present.* New York: Harper and Row.

Sahli, Nancy. (1979, Spring/Summer). "Sexuality in 19th and 20th Century America: The Sources and Their Problems." *Radical History Review,* 20:89-96.

Shepard, M. (1940). *Our Enchanted Island.* Edgartown, MA: Dukes County Historical Society.

Showalter, Elaine, ed. (1978). *These Modern Women.* Westbury, NY: Feminist Press.

Sipley, L.W. (1957). *A Collector's Guide to American Photography.* Philadelphia.

Sklar, Kathryn Kish. (1975, Fall). "American Female Historians in Context, 1770-1930." *Feminist Studies,* 3 (1/2):171-84.

Smith, Daniel Scott. (1974). "Family Limitation, Sexual Control, and Domestic Feminism in Victorian America." In Mary Hartman, and Lois Banner, eds., *Clio's Consciousness Raised.* New York: Harper Torch.

Smith-Rosenburg, Carroll. (1975). "The Female World of Love and Ritual." *Signs,* 1:1-29.

Sochen, June. (1974). *Herstory: A Woman's View of American History.* New York: Alfred.

Steichen, E., ed. (1962). *The Bitter Years, 1935-41: Rural America as Seen by the Photographers of the Farm Security Administration.* New York: Museum of Modern Art.

Stowe, Lyman Beecher. (1934). *Saints, Sinners and Beechers.* New York: Blue Ribbon.

Taft, R. (1938). *Photography and the American Scene: A Social History, 1839-1889.* New York: Macmillian.

Tassin, Algernon. (1916). *The Magazine in America.* New York: Dodd, Mead.

Temple Grove Seminary. (1882). *Year Book.* Saratoga Springs, NY: Author.

Thomas, Alan. (1978). *The Expanding Eye. Photography and the Nineteenth-Century Mind.* London: Croom Helm.

Thoreau, H.D. (1896). *Cape Cod,* 2 vols. Boston and New York: Houghton Mifflin. Ill. AMW.

————. (1961). *A Yankee in Canada.* Montreal: Harvest House.

Van Why, Joseph S. (1975). *Nook Farm.* Hartford: Stowe-Day Foundation.

Welter, Barbara. (1966, Summer). "The Cult of True Womanhood, 1820-1860." *American Quarterly,* 18:151-74.

"What Settlers Say about Manitoba and the Northwest Territory." (1886, April 22). Winnipeg: *Manitoba Free Press.*

Who Was Who in America, vol. 3, 1951-60. Chicago: Marquis-Who's Who, 1960.

Wood, J.P. (1949). *Magazines in the United States.* New York: Ronald Press.

They seek a country

WORKING LIGHT

Designed and composed by Carrie Colton Graphic Design, Ottawa, ON

Printed and bound by Love Printing Service Ltd., Stittsville, ON

Typeset in Perpetua

Printed on Repap Matte, cover 80lb, text 100lb

CARLETON UNIVERSITY PRESS